Passion, Persistence, and Patience

Passion, Persistence, and Patience

Key Skills for Achieving Project Success

Alfonso Bucero

BEP BUSINESS EXPERT PRESS

Passion, Persistence, and Patience: Key Skills for Achieving Project Success

Copyright © Business Expert Press, LLC, 2019.

First published in 2019 by
Business Expert Press, LLC
222 East 46th Street, New York, NY 10017
www.businessexpertpress.com

ISBN-13: 978-1-94819-868-4 (paperback)
ISBN-13: 978-1-94819-869-1 (e-book)

Business Expert Press Portfolio and Project Management Collection

Collection ISSN: 2156-8189 (print)
Collection ISSN: 2156-8200 (electronic)

Cover and interior design by Exeter Premedia Services Private Ltd., Chennai, India

First edition: 2019

10 9 8 7 6 5 4 3 2 1

Printed in the United States of America.

Dedication

I wanted to thank my best friend Randall L. Englund for his encouragement to write this book. He always helped me with his feedback, comments, and advice along my professional life. This book is also dedicated to three different project influencers:

- All upper managers, executives, and project managers practitioners who helped me directly or indirectly to get this project happen, contributing with their opinions, criticism, experiences, and real practices.
- To my editor who sponsored me on this project, offering their commitment and support from the start to the end of this project.
- To my wife, Rose, who always supported and encouraged me to get this project finished.
- To my two sons and daughter who always encouraged me to move forward.
- To Dr. Ralf Müller who encouraged me to finish my PhD and opened my mind to the academic world.

I encourage you to share with me your opinions, ideas, feedback, and real stories in order to improve futures editions of this book. Today is a good day to start reading it, but I am sure that tomorrow will be even better.

Abstract

A number of research studies about project manager skills needed in the future say that soft, or people, skills are core necessities during the next 10 years at least. Enthusiasm, persistence, and patience of the project managers are three key skills to achieve more successful projects in organizations. All best practice recommendations and key success criteria point to the importance of keeping enthusiasm, being persistent, and cultivating and exerting your patience, but few sources exist about how to develop those skills.

The aim of this book is to inspire and encourage project practitioners, executives, and beginners in the project management field and to develop passion, persistence, and patience inside them in order to be contagious with project stakeholders in organizations. The target audience are project managers, project leaders, and facilitators. The second audience are executives or managers who are, or will be, sponsors of a project or program. In reality, almost everybody does projects of some sort and will benefit from the guidelines presented.

This book portends a positive impact on project practitioners through sharing real examples, case studies, and checklists. The ideas and stories being told intend to help a reader increase his or her enthusiasm in managing projects, become aware of the need to insist and be perseverant when managing team members and other project stakeholders, and cultivate his or her patience through practices offered by the author.

Keywords

communication; dedication; effort; enthusiasm; influence; leadership; passion; patience; persistence; soft skills; teamwork

Contents

Foreword

Little did I know that a decision I needed to make in 1992 would have a huge impact for me over the next quarter century. As chair for an internal project management conference at Hewlett-Packard Company, I had reviewers' inputs for proposed papers submitted by practicing project managers. One paper in particular was on the borderline—it came from a Spanish author whose English was clearly not his native language and reviewers gave it marginal scores. I sensed there was something valuable in the content and so accepted the paper to be presented. The author, Alfonso Bucero, went on to work hard on his presentation and writing skills and managed to consistently share his passion, persistence, and patience about the project management profession. He also became a customer, client, and colleague for the HP Project Management Initiative, where I worked at the time. Now, I claim Alfonso as co-author, co-facilitator, and best friend.

When editing chapters for *Creating the Project Office: A Manager's Guide to Leading Organizational Change*, Dr. Robert J. Graham and I pondered what made Alfonso's chapter, "Implementing the Project Office: Case Study," so valuable. Was there one thing he did that constituted success for the Spanish project office he implemented? No. What he did was practice passion, persistence, and patience. His examples amply illustrated how these traits guided him to address real-life challenges and opportunities.

Having worked with Alfonso now for many years, I believe I have come to know the man and his works. However, every time I read one of his books or blogs, I learn something new. This is a remarkable skill—continuously learning innovative ideas and practices and articulating why and how to implement them through the stories he tells. This book about his 3P's is no exception.

Values that Alfonso and I share in common is that all leaders need to create healthy environments for people to consistently and sustainably achieve project success; sponsors can do a better job of guiding and supporting project teams; and project managers can expand their people skills. An organic approach to project management means people adapt effective concepts from nature to make organizations more project-friendly, leading to greater value-added and economic results. All this comes together when project managers become more complete through adopting, adapting, and applying skills from multiple disciplines.

Alfonso's thought leadership, educational offerings, and writings are timeless contributions, providing lessons that enhance and carry others throughout their careers. His works withstand the test of time, and his message keeps evolving about environments, competencies, and attributes required to meet the dynamic needs and direction of the future of project management. He presents, consults, coaches, and mentors project managers and executives, focusing on people skills and creating environments for successful projects. He especially focuses on a positive attitude as a huge factor in personal effectiveness. Yes, *today is a good day* and *tomorrow will be better* when the lessons shared by Alfonso are firmly rooted in everyday actions.

His books and seminars continue to delight readers and audiences by providing a systematic, energetic, and inclusive focus on the set of skills and attitude needed for success when managing today's projects. The message is powerful and clearly articulated. It applies to emerging and experienced project managers alike. As you read this book and apply its principles, I believe you will be inspired to broaden and deepen your skills to the point of achieving more project success more of the time.

I thank Alfonso for letting me share my comments and provide my points of view on the subject. Believe me, he has written a precious book. I wish your reading to be as useful and inspiring to you as it is for me. I encourage you to put the thoughts into action; reap the benefits derived from personal effectiveness and move forward to improve project management in every aspect of your life.

Randall L. Englund, Executive Consultant
October 2018
Englund Project Management Consultancy
St. George, Utah, USA
www.englundpmc.com

Introduction

Why to write a book about passion, persistence, and patience? Because it has been my motto over the years, because I believe in that, and I felt the need to share my experiences about it with the project management community. Over the years, I have managed different projects and without being conscious of it, I was contagious to many people through my passion, persistence, and patience, working on the project management business, contributing as a professional association volunteer, and delivering public talks worldwide.

The behavior and reactions you have in your job, at home, and with your colleagues and friends has an impact on the lives of the people around you. You, as a project manager, need to be enthusiastic, persistent, and develop patience in order to get good project results. In fact, if you want to make a positive impact on your projects, you need to be enthusiastic with all your project stakeholders. That way people will feel better valued and loved by you. Without enthusiasm, there cannot be good project performance. If you are a project manager, you need to be enthusiastic with your team because if not you will demotivate them. No matter what your professional or personal goals are in life, or what you want to accomplish, you can achieve them faster, you can be more effective, and the contribution you make can last longer if you learn how to become an enthusiastic person, getting across enthusiasm.

Your Passion

I have observed that passion is very curious. Even though we can affect almost everyone around us, our level of influence is not the same with everyone. For example, when you have a team meeting with your team members and present an idea to them or suggest, do they all respond in the same way? Of course, not. One person may think all your ideas are inspiring. Another may view everything you say with skepticism. You can identify which one you have to influence over. On the other hand, the skeptic who resisted your idea may be more accepting to it if it were presented by an executive.

If you pay attention to people's responses to yourself and others, you can see that people respond to one another according to their level of enthusiasm. I consider passion like a specific application of influence. Passion does not come to us instantaneously; it grows by stages.

We are influenced by what we see. Several times I had the opportunity to share with an audience of more than hundred people my experiences as a Project Management Institute (PMI) volunteer, and I spoke with all my energy for one hour. I never get tired when I am enjoying what I do, and I love speaking on public. Many of the attendees approached me after my speech and gave me their business card to keep in touch with me. Some of them said, "you made my day." I was touched. It has not been the first time that happened to me. We are able to generate positive emotions on people not because we are great, just because we really believe and do what we preach. I always encourage people at professional congresses to participate and present their experiences in front of others. I always tell people about my experience presenting my first paper on project management in an international congress and how the reaction of the attendees encouraged me to continue presenting again and again and again.

Enthusiastic people give value to other people. I don't know what kind of enthusiasm for the profession you have today when you are reading this book. Your actions may touch the lives of hundreds of people, or perhaps your enthusiasm may be infective for two or three team members or colleagues. The number of people is not what is most important. The key point is to remember that your level of influence is not static. I want to help you become a project manager of high enthusiasm. You can have an incredibly positive impact on the lives of others. You can give a lot of value to them.

I don't know exactly what your dream is in life or what kind of legacy you want to leave. But if you want to make an impact and develop a passion for your profession, insist again and again if you believe your aimed objective is achievable and apply your patience to achieve it. You can do it because you are excellent. I mean if you believe you will be able to exceed your project stakeholder's expectations.

Definitions

I found several definitions of passion from different authors: the first one was the state of being acted upon or affected by something external, especially something alien to something alien to one's nature or one's customary behavior. Another definition is a strong or extravagant fondness, enthusiasm, or desire for anything. My definition of passion is the feeling of positive desire to achieve your aims.

Persistence may be defined as the willingness to keep going even when the odds are bad and our enthusiasm has waned; or the fact of continuing in an opinion or course of action in spite of difficulty or opposition. My definition is never giving up when you believe you can achieve your goals.

The definition of patience is the capacity to accept or tolerate delay, problems, or suffering without becoming annoyed or anxious; or the bearing of provocation, annoyance, misfortune, or pain, without complaint, loss of temper, irritation, or the like. My definition of patience is to deal with life without losing your temper and with positive attitude.

I need to say that all three concepts play in concert and I applied it during my life and professional career. They worked and are still working for me. Try it and you will learn something.

Book Structure

This book integrates different pieces to develop and sustain passion, persistence and patience as a project manager.

Outline

Each chapter highlights thoughts and real stories about a particular subject linked to my 3Ps (passion, persistence, and patience). Here is an outline of what is covered:

- Introduction
- Chapter 1: This chapter introduces the concepts of passion, persistence, and patience and how they have been part of my skill set as a project practitioner over the years managing

projects in organizations. At the end of this chapter, an assessment tool is provided.

- Chapter 2: Explains how to develop passion, persistence, and patience for personal, project, and organizational success, sharing real stories and case studies. An action plan preparation is explained by the end of this chapter.
- Chapter 3: How to sustain and maintain passion, persistence, and patience is clearly explained in this chapter. Through exercises and real stories, the reader will be able to sustain those skills for achieving successful projects.
- Chapter 4: This chapter give you clues, suggestions, and ideas about how to be contagious and infect people positively being more enthusiastic, having more persistence, and developing more patience. An assessment tool is included in this chapter.
- Chapter 5: How to learn something from anybody else is the focus of this chapter. Learning from peers, colleagues, bosses, and customers. This chapter explains the concept of learning from anybody every day.
- Chapter 6: This chapter is focused on how to get your relationships growing up because the development of your three Ps (passion, persistence, and patience). An assessment tool is also provided in this chapter.
- Chapter 7: Develop your professional career, working on your professional vision. Planning for your professional career success is the purpose of this chapter.
- Chapter 8: Use your courage and assess it. Go beyond your comfort zone and development of your courage are explained in this chapter.
- Chapter 9: This chapter is focused on taking action, reviewing your plan, and just doing it. In this chapter, some "never give up" best practices are told.
- Chapter 10: Summary and conclusions and preparing an "action plan."

Through the whole book, I'll be emphasizing the importance of being positive and developing a positive attitude when trying to develop your

3Ps skills as a project manager. All the best practices and ideas shared in this book are based on my particular experience and on my interaction with other project professionals worldwide. Only I am responsible of the content of this book.

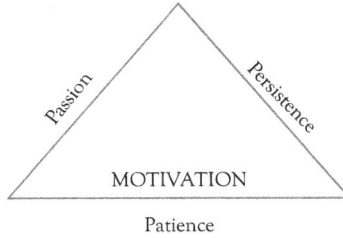

Patience

You will be familiar with the iron triangle, also known as a triple constrains for a project. I want to define my motivation triangle for project success. The sides of my triangle are: Passion, Persistence, and Patience. These are three basic skills to be developed in order to be motivated and motivate your project team members and stakeholders. It takes time and practice, but you can do it because you need to be *excellent* as a project practitioner. Did you enjoy your reading so far? I hope so. If your answer is positive, please move forward to Chapter 1. If not, please close the book and try it again tomorrow because I need great professionals like you are who are able to give me feedback about the use of 3Ps.

CHAPTER 1

Passion, Persistence, and Patience

Success consists of going from failure to failure without loss of enthusiasm.

—Winston Churchill

Long time ago I adopted passion, persistence and patience as my motto. Perhaps because everything I did in my life needed to use, develop, and sustain those qualities. I was born in a Spanish family, not a rich one, but with the support I needed. I was constantly observed and the center of attention of my relatives as I was growing up, had a happy childhood, attended a good school and learned French as my second language. I always was passionate about reading, learning, and researching on new subjects. My scores at the primary school were very good, so my parents always supported me when I asked for a book, training course or something related to learn. In fact, my father was always very supportive on that subject, he believed that I needed to be well prepared for my future and he encouraged me to be focused on being trained and educated to get a University degree.

Everything was great during Primary and Secondary School but when I started to study at the University, I started to fail some times and I learned from failure to failure. I did not pass the first time in some subjects, so as I had the enthusiasm to move forward and, needed to use my persistence and my patience to progress in order to obtain my degree. That was not a path of roses, it was challenging and difficult but I was determined to do it. My degree consisted of five calendar years plus the final degree project. It took me seven years because I got a job at the third year of my studies, so I had less time to study and needed to develop my discipline and persistence to keep going on. It was the first time I was conscious of when you have passion about something, persistence and patience need to be cultivated to achieve your goal.

After a couple of years working for a multinational organization in Spain I discovered that project management was my passion. I believe passion is a priceless quality that makes everything different in our lives (Bucero 2010). Professional life is always difficult and challenging but when you have passion for your profession, that enthusiasm raises your excitement and interest to move forward. It has happened to me during my whole life. And that is the main reason why I am writing this book. I strongly believe that you need to convert your dreams into reality. You can do it without any doubt only if you believe you can. That is the principle I have been following as a professional during the last 37 years and it worked for me, so why not for you. I hope my real stories about my 3 Ps will help you to reflect and learn to build up a better future.

Passion

I truly believe passion makes the difference between success and failure in our lives. In 1997, Steve Jobs returned to Apple after a 12-year absence. The company he had cofounded was running out of cash and close to bankruptcy. Jobs held a staff meeting and explained the role passion would play in revitalizing the brand:

> *Apple is not about making boxes for people to get their jobs done, although we do that well. Apple is about something more. Its core value is that we believe that people with passion can change the world for the better.*

The simple phrase—"people with passion can change the world" (Entrepreneur Network July 2015)—holds the secret to entrepreneurial success. Many times your body language shows your emotions (Figure 1.1). Several years later, in 2005, Jobs returned to the theme in his famous commencement speech at Stanford University. "You've got to find what you love," Jobs said. "The only way to do great work is to love what you do. If you have not found it yet, keep looking. Do not settle. As with all matters of the heart, you will know when you find it."

What Passion Can Do for You?

Passion is very important. Following your passion is the secret to overcoming the setbacks all entrepreneurs face and it builds strengths and

Figure 1.1 Passion for project management

resistance against the inevitable naysayers who will question your vision. I still remember when I left Hewlett-Packard in 2002 many of my colleagues told me sentences like*: "where are you going Alfonso, you have a safe job here" or: "It is raining cat and dogs outside, business is very difficult to be able to survive," or "you are bad on sales, you will fail." My answer was "I love you too."* I started a new company focused on my passion (project management). So, I did not care of the "naysayers" and I survived, I achieved my vision and created a Project Management Consulting company where I am still working for sixteen years ago. It is also an essential ingredient in successful communication. If you are not passionate about your ideas, nobody else will be. I believe that every professional needs to have a purpose (Englund and Bucero 2012), my purpose is: *"to help organizations to change their attitude to achieve better project and organizational success"*

When I created my own company on 2002 I reflected about the "why." I mean, why did I need to start up a company working on project management? My answer was: because I needed to help companies to understand better the project management discipline in order to manage better and better projects for organizational success. I had passion to do that, I worked on designing and implementing a portfolio of products and services every year. On 2010 the financial crisis affected my company results and I lost some money. My passion for project management was there, I understood that I needed to make a difference on the market.

Then I defined my company purpose as: *To help organizations to develop and sustain a positive attitude managing projects for organizational success.*

As an entrepreneur I am passionate—but not about the products I sell and deliver to my customers, but about purpose and mission. I am passionate about changing the world or disrupting an established category. For example, Steve Jobs was not passionate about computer hardware. He was passionate about building tools that would help people unleash their personal creativity. "Someone who is passionate will immerse themselves in a field. They want to know everything they can about it," says Francisco García, the founder of -A-Hair Stylist Workshop. In a recent conversation, Francisco told me how much he admired Steve Jobs as someone who followed his passions, wherever they would lead.

Francisco said that passion is a fundamental trait he looks for when deciding who to hire for his business. He listens carefully to the words people use. There's no rush to create a business you're not passionate about just to be rich, he said. It will not work in the long run. You need to have your heart in it. The heart is what's going to drive you to make the most money. Follow your passion and make a difference.

I do this passion activity all the time in my workshops, projects, and events (a picture of me talking and smiling is shown in Figure 1.2). I get

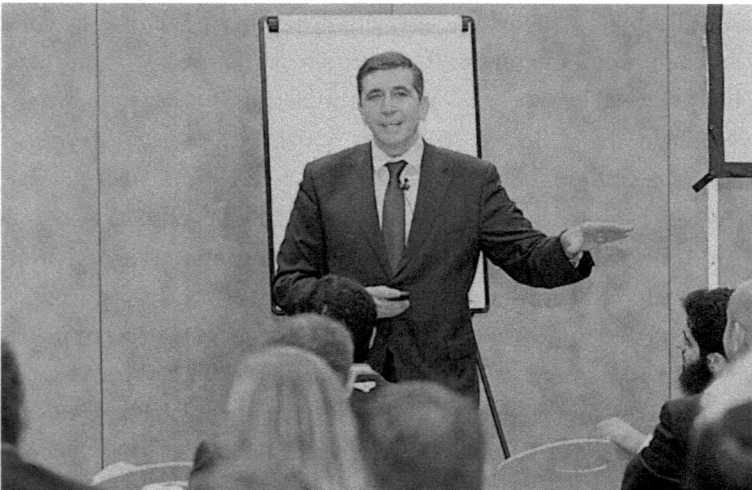

Figure 1.2 Alfonso Bucero showing his passion in a public talk

on stage and I speak and facilitate with excitement, energy, and passion. One of the exercises I do, in order to demonstrate that passion is important, is just to change my communication style for a while. I become dull, bored and show a true lack of passion and energy. It is amazing to see everyone's reaction in the room. They hate it! I do this to demonstrate why passion matters. We have something called Mirror Neurons. We automatically pick up the emotions of others.[1] Have you experienced sitting in your office and someone who has had a crap morning has just walked it and literally lumped it all over the office. They have been cranky, down or upset; and the whole energy in the room has changed. I am sure you felt it.

Passion is about believing in what you do, inspiring others to believe in it, and loving why you do what you do. Simon Sinek who wrote one of my favorite books "Start with Why"[2] said—"*People don't buy what you do, they buy why you do it.*" And I verified that on the delivery of my services as a PM consultant. I always take care of the people around me to get across the message of enthusiasm on everything I do. I do not need to make any special effort because it is natural, is coming from my mindset.

What Inspires Your Employees or Project Stakeholders?

Everything is about people—us, the individuals. Everyone needs to get personally inspired. Having a clear, common dream and purpose that every employee can identify with is the best way to motivate. Passion requires courage, even young-like energy, to keep your eyes on your goal and do all you can to achieve it.

This is exactly how you need to see your staff: as individuals and, first of all, human beings. As a leader, your task is to inspire and encourage positive attitude rather than to be a mere supervisor, as cited in

---

[1] Totterdell, P., K. Niven, and D. Holman. 2010. "Our Emotional Neighbourhood—How Social Networks Can Regulate What We Feel." *The Psychologist* 23, pp. 474–77.
[2] Sinek, S. 2009. *Start With Why: How Great Leaders Inspire Everyone To Take Action.* New York, NY: Portfolio.

Figure 1.3 Smell the inspiration

Figure 1.3. Ask your people to smile more. I remind them that every day in the morning when they are brushing their teeth the need to smile and repeat "I am excellent." Please smile more and more every day and you will enjoy much more moments in your life. Furthermore, you will show your happiness to anybody else and be contagious.

Why Should You Measure Passion?

What you cannot measure, you cannot lead! (Zak 2009). This well-known fact also applies to passion. If you want to see enthusiasm as one of your goals, you also need to decide how you will measure it.

One main reason to measure your passion is that it inspires the whole staff to rethink their level of passion. When the staff's focus is on passion and on how to increase it, the level will increase for sure. Soon the whole staff will start to think new ways to strengthen their enthusiasm or passion together. Passion is contagious. Please ask yourself:

- What is the level of passion do I have in the tasks, or in the project am I managing?
- Is that level enough or can you improve it?

The answer to those questions will give you some clues, about what is the amount of passion you are putting at work. Measure your passion temperature and you will always discover some ways to improve.

How Can You Measure Your Passion?

The aim of a passion survey needs to focused on the following subjects:

- Measuring the present state of passion
- Understanding the factors effecting passion and prioritizing them
- Increasing passion at the workplace

Measuring passion needs to be attached to already existing processes. In practice, this means that measuring is continuous, results are followed in some common meeting and the points for improvement are actually put into practice.

Every company can decide the most suitable cycle for their measuring. It is important, however, that measuring is continuous. In general, the survey is worthwhile to complete at least once a month to actually keep track of how things are going. As the whole staff answers the survey once a month, the survey should not be too long. And the questions need to be considered precisely.

What to Ask?

The target of a survey is always an individual—that is, the survey measures every individual's passion separately. Good themes to cover are individual's passion for their work tasks, and their sense of freedom, responsibility and inspiration.

Some suggested questions are:

1. Does your staff feel energetic and passionate at work?
2. Do they work on tasks which bring them joy, accomplishments and challenges?
3. Do they have the chance to work in a flow state, without interruptions and giving their whole effort?
4. Do they feel proud of their work, the company's vision and future?

When the results are ready, the first thing to focus on needs to be the factors increasing passion: the ones that are best fulfilled and are considered to be the most important factors by your staff. You need to try to focus on understanding why those factors have such an impact on passion.

When you have the facts on which factors increase passion, and why, it is time to consider the obstacles standing in the way of inspiration. You need to choose one or a maximum of two challenges and aim at solving the reasons for why they decrease passion.

The best way to gain true understanding is to have a discussion about the results openly with all of your project stakeholders. The discussion needs to be held in an open and trusting environment without blaming anyone. It is the only way to make progress and take steps forward, as a one motivated, harmonious and enthusiastic team. Now, it is time to measure your staff's passion.

How to Assess Your People Passion

The following questions will help you to assess the level of passion you or you people have:

1. What's your dream job?
2. Why are you applying for this position?
3. What do you love to do?
4. What do you dislike?
5. Where do you see yourself in five-year time?
6. Tell me about a time in your current or previous work where you were intensely motivated? Where you were bored?
7. What things in life do you do where you lose track of time?
8. Why have you chosen this industry to work in? (Do they show an interest in your industry and company?)
9. What research have they done on your company?
10. Do they display general enthusiasm and eagerness to learn and try new things?

The crucial thing here is to watch where the person lights up/comes to life which is often indicated by faster speech, eyes and body language and so on. Also, when they over talk, it can indicate a subject they are passionate about. If you are dealing with more of an "analytic" as opposed to a more "expressive" person this can be a little harder to gauge.

I want to share a funny story with you that illustrates how significant is to show your passion when are interviewed for a job position. I still remember that interview when I needed to hire a new software programmer for my project team. He was a little bit nervous but very assertive in his answers to my questions but, when I asked him: what do you dislike earlier in the morning? He said the main think I do not like in the morning is to get up to go for work. He made me laugh, I could not avoid it. He was not passionate about his potential job, so I decided not to hire him.

Persistence

One of the definitions of persistence is the fact of continuing in an opinion or course of action in spite of difficulty or opposition (Mukwevho 2013). Others define it like the fact of persist or the quality to insist. Being persistent is a skill that can help you to achieve a goal, get what you wish and can even be a means by which you assert yourself in the face of stubborn or difficult people.

The application of persistence to any task, interaction or goal is often what distinguishes between those who are successful and those who fail in any endeavor. Indeed, a lack of persistence or "giving up too soon" is one of the most common reasons for failure in any endeavor. We are complex creatures. Hope and anguish can coexist and still create something truly amazing. Persistence is the ability to maintain action regardless of your feelings. You press on even when you feel like quitting, until you achieve that important goal. I surprise myself every day.

People give up too soon because they have wrong expectations of themselves and the outcome. They expect the way to be easy, and they are surprised when they find the reality to be the opposite. Their enthusiasm quickly melts and they lose heart. Then, start your journey with the right expectation. And don't underestimate the amount of time required either.

Let me share with you one of examples of persistence: I am PMP (Project Management Professional) certified but I did not pass the PMP exam the first time. I was so arrogant my first time and thought that I

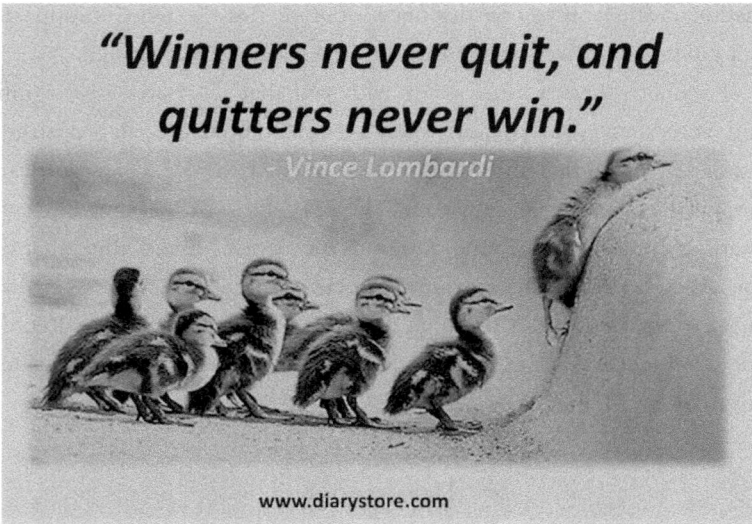

Figure 1.4 Winners never quit

did need not study just because I had 15 years of project management experience and, thought it would be enough to pass but it was not. I tried again a second time because I had it as a clear professional objective to be certified, but I was managing a project far away home and started to study very late every day, getting fall sleep most of the days, so I did not pass the second time I tried it. Finally, I passed the exam the third time because I studied enough and, dedicated effort and time (winners never quit as showed in Figure 1.4.

Remember, there is no such thing as cheap success. Expect a hard way, not an easy one, and you will be mentally prepared when you encounter the reality. The size of your commitment should be proportional to the size of your desire. You will be blown away by what you can achieve if you don't lose hope in yourself. Einstein persisted and stayed with problems longer to make sure he found exactly what he was looking for. He once said "It's not that I'm so smart, it's just that I stay with problems longer."

What Persistence Can Do for You?

Being persistent can contribute to personal and professional success, but you need to be sure that you are dealing with achievable objectives.

Persistence, has a lot to do with your success in life and business. Persistence is omnipotent. Calvin Coolidge once said "The slogan *press on* has solved and always will solve the problems of the human race." Talent and genius cannot take the place of persistence. The value of persistence comes from a vision of the future that's so compelling you would give almost anything to make it real.

Persistence of action comes from persistence of vision. When you're super-clear about what you want in such a way that your vision doesn't change much, you'll be more consistent—and persistent—in your actions. And that consistency of action will produce consistency of results. Every obstacle is an opportunity to improve.

> *I will persist until I succeed. Always will I take another step. If that is of no avail I will take another, and yet another. In truth, one step at a time is not too difficult. I know that small attempts, repeated, will complete any undertaking.*
>
> —Mandino, 2007

When you work on any big goal, your motivation can wax and wane. Sometimes you'll feel motivated; sometimes you won't. But it's not your motivation that will produce results—it's your action. The decision to persist. To make progress even when you don't feel like it. Persistence allows you to keep taking action even when you don't feel motivated to do so, and therefore you keep accumulating results.

On March 2006 I started my studies to get a MSc in project management by the Zaragoza University. It took me three years instead of two because I am a business man always travelling across the oceans, but I had a clear objective of accomplishing my goals and used my persistence spending one more year than planned to achieve my MSc, and I got it by the end of 2008. By the end of 2009 I decided to study to obtain my PhD but I was not able to be registered at the University because of a big workload that year. On 2010 I was registered as a PhD student and I defended my project on July 2011, then I got the license to research on 2012. During 2013 and 2014 I tried to advance on my research but my thesis supervisor did not give me enough or right support, so I got lost and demotivated. Every time I met my supervisor he told me: "*Alfonso you will never achieve your PhD because is not your first priority.*"

That situation forced me to move to another university (MU). Then I restarted my research at that University on 2015, it seemed that I would get the support I needed. My mentor was better, I continued traveling outside my country of residence and I was not able to advance as much as I wanted. Finally, by June 2017 I had to present my thesis report but I did not get enough data from my surveys according to the University requirements. I was frustrated because I had worked a lot on that and I felt much more focused on my objective. Then that University did not allow me to continue. For a couple of months, I was demotivated but I reflected upon, contacted some colleagues who already have a PhD and I am now registered in ISM University.

In only two months my concentration, understanding and focus have changed positively. My supervisor is encouraging me all the time and now I know that I will achieve my objective. It is clearer now, so what I need is hard work and good supervision to achieve my goal. After four months with that supervisor I was able to submit my first research paper to an International Research Conference, and two months later I was notified that my paper was accepted thanks to the support and encouragement received from him. He made a difference because he explained very clearly how to write a research paper. It took me some time because my background is not academic but I did it.

What Inspires Your Employees or Project Stakeholders?

People who persists no matter the obstacles, sooner or later are bound to succeed. Despite the setbacks, it's in your best interest to turn obstacles into stepping stones. Don't choose to complain, or worse, to just give up (Bucero 2010). These choices do nothing to get you across the finish line. When your team members or other project stakeholders have clear objectives and expectations giving up is not an option. If I had to select one quality, one personal characteristic that I regard as being highly related with success, whatever the field, I would pick the trait of persistence. A lack of persistence or "giving up too soon" is one of the most common reasons for failure in any endeavor. A little more persistence, a little more effort is sometimes what you need to get closer to the goal. Once you create a belief that there is an obstacle you cannot overcome, you stop looking for solutions.

The greater the achievement you seek, the more likely you will persist to achieve it. I always defended that "ambition is the path to success. Persistence is the vehicle you arrive in." Persistence in the service of a higher goal calls out many other virtues in you. You will push yourself to beyond what is comfortable to achieve your chosen goal. And you should know why you want your goal in the first place. And your why must be bigger than the obstacles. The bigger your "why" the better. Persistent people have a goal or vision in mind that motivates and drives them. Reaching this goal becomes the focal point of their life and they devote a greater percentage their energies and time toward reaching it. To stay persistent, break that big goal down into smaller pieces. Smaller pieces are easier to manage and easier to accomplish, and they'll give you a feeling of accomplishment sooner.

In one project I managed in Granada (South of Spain) I had fifteen project stakeholders. Several of them were resistant because nobody informed them about how the change that project was provoking would be affecting them in their jobs and positions. As a project manager I needed to get as many allies as possible to be successful in that project. Then I used my persistence explaining to them one by one how much their organization needed the contribution of everyone. I found resistance because of political interests among some of them, but again I spent a lot of time with them treating them for dinner or having some Spanish tapas from time to time. It was very hard at the beginning but after a couple of months everybody was understanding that all of us were doing a special effort in the benefit of the project. Using my persistence in this real case was one of the keys for project success. Most of my project stakeholders were business unit managers and finally through my persistence I got them working as a team.

Why Should You Measure Persistence?

Because many people give up so soon. Then you need to measure how many times you are still pursuing your goal, failing and trying it again.

Persistence is important in your life as a project practitioner and you need to measured (see Figure 1.5). It will mark how well you accomplish tasks that you set for yourself. It will determine whether you are going to finish or quit before you have actually reached your goal (Vujicic 2011).

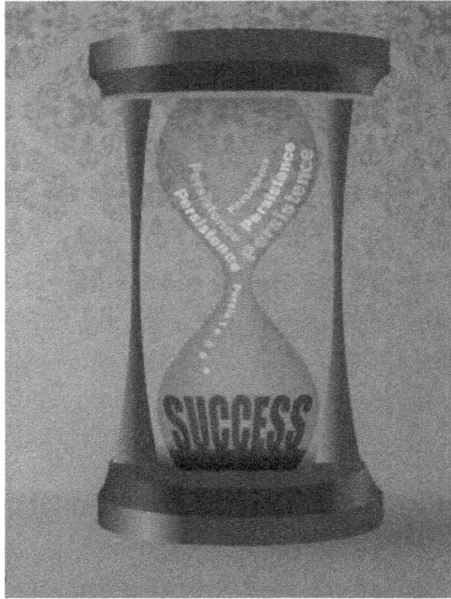

Figure 1.5 Measuring persistence

You may have many great ideas for your business, projects or personal life. However, if you do not have persistence to see them through, it is a waste of time to get started. Do you know how to measure your degree of persistence? Before beginning any task or setting a goal, you need to understand your level of persistence and commitment. It is not exactly easy to measure your own persistence. If you are going to be honest with yourself, the only way to measure your persistence is during a task. Then you can measure your persistence level based on when or if you give up. This could take days, weeks, months, and even years. Most people do not have that much time to waste just to find out their persistence levels. Instead you can ask yourself a few questions that can help you figure out your level of persistence.

How Can You Measure It?

Cal Newport over at Study Hacks, wrote an interesting article where he claims that "getting started is overrated" (Newport 2008). He argues that too many people get started without commitment. As a result, they waste valuable time and energy on pursuits that they will give up after a few months of haphazard effort. Action without persistence is a waste of time. Continuing from Cal's idea, I think it's useful to ask yourself what your level of commitment is to a project or goal before starting. Measuring persistence is not easy. The only true way to know your persistence level is to work on a project and see when you give up. If you quit a goal after two years, your degree of persistence is two years.

Unfortunately, most of us do not have years of our lives to waste just to measure the level of commitment to a new project. Although it won't measure the real thing, I think there is a thought experiment that comes pretty close to pinpointing the actual value. Are you willing to work forever? Pick any goal you want to measure your persistence for. Now, ask yourself how long you would be willing to work on the goal, without any positive feedback. How long would you be willing to work on a project, without being able to see any results from your efforts?

That length of time, I believe, is a rough estimate of your commitment to a project. Notice I didn't ask how long you would be willing to work on a project. Instead, I asked, how long you would be able to work in a vacuum, devoid of any knowledge that you were making progress. If you want to get in shape, ask yourself how long you would be willing to go to the gym every day, if you didn't lose a single pound, didn't increase at all in strength, or didn't look any different. How long would you be willing to last?

If you want to start a business, ask yourself how long you would be willing to keep experimenting and producing without earning a single dollar of revenue. Or receiving any indication that your business would continue. Persisting Forever is Stupid (Young 2016). Obviously, working forever without any results means you're doing something wrong. Either you've picked an impossible pursuit (try flying by flapping your arms) or your approach is completely broken.

However, as a thought experiment, this question is still valuable. There are going to be periods in the pursuit of any goal, where you will completely lack positive feedback. You won't have any motivational fuel to encourage you forward. The question is based on how long you feel you can continue in spite of this total absence of results.

How to Assess Persistence

In order to evaluate how persistent, you are, ask yourself the following questions:

1. When the going gets tough do you keep going?
2. Do you see projects through to completion… even when the process becomes boring or monotonous?
3. When you hit roadblocks, do you hang in there to find a solution?

Let's just be frank here for a moment. Being persistent is not easy. In fact, very often it is hard. It's often so much easier and sometimes more appealing to give up. Think about the last time you went on a fitness kick. You're doing really well … then winter arrives and the allure of the warm done and an extra half hour in bed is so much more inviting than the wet, dark and cold morning. Those who persist (and yes, I admire you) end up with the health, fitness and vitality that we were striving for in the beginning when the motivation was high and the weather warm.

Patience

What is the meaning of patience? It can be defined as the quality of being patient, as the bearing of provocation, annoyance, misfortune, or pain, without complaint, loss of temper, irritation, or the like. I also found it as an ability or willingness to suppress restlessness or annoyance when confronted with delay: to have patience with a slow learner.

Many good things really do come to those who wait. Having patience means being able to wait calmly in the face of frustration or adversity, so anywhere there is frustration or adversity we have the opportunity to practice it (see Figure 1.6). Yet patience is essential to daily life—and

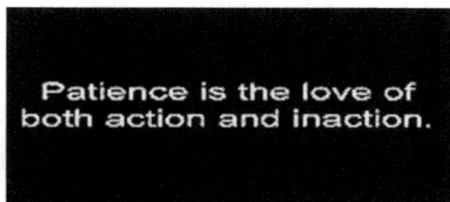

Figure 1.6 *Patience*

might be key to a happy one. Having patience means being able to wait calmly in the face of frustration or adversity, so anywhere there is frustration or adversity—for example, nearly everywhere—we have the opportunity to practice it. At home with our kids, at work with our colleagues, at the grocery store with half our city's population, patience can make the difference between annoyance and equanimity, between worry and tranquility. Religions and philosophers have long praised the virtue of patience; now researchers are starting to do so as well. Recent studies have found that, sure enough, good things really do come to those who wait. Some of these science-backed benefits are detailed in the following, along with three ways to cultivate more patience in your life.

The Stanford marshmallow experiment was a series of studies on "delayed gratification" in the late 1960s and early 1970s led by psychologist Walter Mischel, then a professor at "Stanford University. In these studies, a child was offered a choice between one small reward provided immediately or two small rewards if they waited for a short period, approximately 15 minutes, during which the tester left the room and then returned. (The reward was sometimes a marshmallow, but often a cookie). In follow-up studies, the researchers found that children who were able to wait longer for the preferred rewards tended to have better life outcomes. A replication attempt with a more diverse sample population over 10 times larger than the original study failed to support the original study's conclusions and suggested that economic background rather than willpower explained the results.

As a project practitioner I found that the organizational environment factors may also help to increase or decrease your patience as a project manager.

What Patience Can Do for You?

This finding is probably easy to believe if you call to mind the stereotypical impatient person: face red, head steaming. And sure enough, according to a 2007 study by Fuller Theological Seminary professor Sarah A. Schnitker and UC Davis psychology professor Robert Emmons, patient people tend to experience less depression and negative emotions, perhaps because they can cope better with upsetting or stressful situations.

They also rate themselves as more mindful and feel more gratitude, more connection to mankind and to the universe, and a greater sense of abundance. I thank God every day for being healthy, having a great family, or even for not gaining a customer proposal but learning from it.

Patience comes in many different stripes. One type is interpersonal patience, which doesn't involve waiting but simply facing annoying people with equanimity. Another type of patience involves waiting out life's hardships without frustration or despair—think of business generation, I have a small company but we need to generate some sales every month to survive in business. There are some months where sales are not coming but we continue seeding and then the flowers grow up, I mean, some sales come. Unsurprisingly, in Schnitker's study, this type of courageous patience was linked to more hope.

Finally, patience over daily hassles— I usually go through traffic jams several mornings per week—seems to go along with good mental health. In particular, people who have this type of patience are more satisfied with life and less depressed.

These studies are good news for people who are already patient, but what about those of us who want to become more patient? In her 2012 study, Schnitker invited 71 undergraduates to participate in two weeks of patience training, where they learned to identify feelings and their triggers, regulate their emotions, empathize with others, and meditate. In two weeks, participants reported feeling more patient toward the trying people in their lives, feeling less depressed, and experiencing higher levels of positive emotions. In other words, patience seems to be a skill you can practice—more on that next—and doing so might bring benefits to your mental health.

Patient people are better friends and neighbors: In relationships with others, patience becomes a form of kindness. Think of the best friend who comforts you night after night over the heartache that just won't go away, or the grandchild who smiles through the story she has heard her grandfather tell countless times. Indeed, research suggests that patient people tend to be more cooperative, more empathic, more equitable, and more forgiving. "Patience involves emphatically assuming some personal discomfort to alleviate the suffering of those around us," write Debra R. Comer and Leslie E. Sekerka in their 2014 study.

Evidence of this is found in a 2008 study that put participants into groups of four and asked them to contribute money to a common pot, which would be doubled and redistributed. The game gave players a financial incentive to be stingy, yet patient people contributed more to the pot than other players did.

This kind of selflessness is found among people with all three types of patience mentioned earlier, not just interpersonal patience: In Schnitker's 2012 study, all three were associated with higher "agreeableness," a personality trait characterized by warmth, kindness, and cooperation. The interpersonally patient people even tended to be less lonely, perhaps because making and keeping friends—with all their quirks and slip-ups—generally requires a healthy dose of patience. "Patience may enable individuals to tolerate flaws in others, therefore displaying more generosity, compassion, mercy, and forgiveness," write Schnitker and Emmons in their 2007 study.

On a group level, patience may be one of the foundations of civil society. Patient people are more likely to vote, an activity that entails waiting months or years for our elected official to implement better policies. Evolutionary theorists believe that patience helped our ancestors survive because it allowed them to do good deeds and wait for others to reciprocate, instead of demanding immediate compensation (which would more likely lead to conflict than cooperation). In that same vein, patience is linked to trust in the people and the institutions around us.

Patience helps us achieve our goals: The road to achievement is a long one, and those without patience—who want to see results immediately—may not be willing to walk it. Think of the recent critiques of millennials for being unwilling to "pay their dues" in an entry-level job, jumping from position to position rather than growing and learning. In her 2012 study, Schnitker also examined whether patience helps students get things done. In five surveys they completed over the course of a semester, patient people of all stripes reported exerting more effort toward their goals than other people did. Those with interpersonal patience in particular made more progress toward their goals and were more satisfied when they achieved them (particularly if those goals were difficult) compared with less patient people. According to Schnitker's analysis, that greater satisfaction with achieving their goals explained why these patient achievers were more content with their lives as a whole.

Patience is linked to good health: The study of patience is still new, but there's some emerging evidence that it might even be good for our health. In their 2007 study, Schnitker and Emmons found that patient people were less likely to report health problems like headaches, acne flair-ups, ulcers, diarrhea, and pneumonia. Other research has found that people who exhibit impatience and irritability—a characteristic of the Type A personality—tend to have more health complaints and worse sleep. If patience can reduce our daily stress, it's reasonable to speculate that it could also protect us against stress's damaging health effects.

What Inspires Your Employees or Project Stakeholders

Patience is connected to trust, hope, faith, love and good character. I found ten Bible verses showing some of the aspects of patience. Being humble, gentle and patient are good skills. You need to be tolerant with your team members but at the same time you need to demonstrate them you have enough authority.

I managed a large project for the Ministry of Work in Spain. I was the project manager who worked for an important multinational firm but all my team members (35) were subcontracted and with a low level of experience. However, all of them had a great attitude and were committed to learn. At the beginning the team performance was really poor. Then I needed to apply my patience with them, listening to them as my first priority. I learned a lot from them about their feelings, as they worked for other company outside their home office and having me as a project manager from a multinational company.

It took me at least three months to start working as a winning team. I allowed them to fail some times because I understood they were unexperienced people, but I gave them feedback every week in a sustained way and they became good team members. I was patient with them understanding that their motivations were not mine. I talked to them face to face so frequently, organized some parties from time to time to tell jokes and laugh for a while together. The project was 18 months long, and by the end of the project I became their real boss because I earned their trust. And the best reward for me was when my team said: "we want to work with you again in the next project."

Why Should You Measure Patience

Obviously, patience has a limit, so you need to measure it, understand what your level is, and prepare a plan to move forward. You need to know the elements that affect your patience to keep it under control. If you, as a project manager, are getting nervous you may affect the level of patience of your team.

As a leader you need to keep your project in control, so you need to develop a high level of patience to manage your project team members and stakeholders.

How Can You Measure Your Patience

In yourself and others, impatience, is easier to determine afterwards. A few instances of not meeting deadlines, and consistently rushing at the last minute, to be somewhere or do something when you have had more than ample time to prepare for it, indicates a chronic lack of patience.

The psychology behind these actions is usually rooted in some sort of internal "impedance"[3] like a fear of failure, or total disinterest and lack of curiosity in the event or thing to be done, or the past experience of finding the thing boring beyond human endurance. If you or another is a very patient person then you are by your natural temperament, already inclined thru genetics, or you have made mental adjustments to the failures you have no doubt experiences when you were not patient, or you have a strong desire to have a very successful outcome in all respects. Pouncing, knee jerking, and other instant reactions, stimulus/response reflexes, are a sure indication of a dearth of patience in our behavior.

One of the dangers I have to lose my patience is when as a project manager I am communicating among my team by oral and written communication and I do not obtain any response. I usually give a couple of

---

[3] **Impedance.** [im-peed-ns] Electricity. the total opposition to alternating current by an electric circuit, equal to the square root of the sum of the squares of the resistance and reactance of the circuit and usually expressed in ohms. Symbol: Z. Impedance | Define Impedance at Dictionary.com
https://dictionary.com/browse/impedance

days to respond my messages but after that when I do not get any news or response I am getting nervous. My reaction is usually trying other method or communicating to other people around it in order to get my message received but it get me crazy some times.

How to Assess Your Patience

I found several questionnaires that try to address how to evaluate your patience. Some of them are very focused on stressing situations and they relate patience with the level of stress you can manage.

As a project manager you need to cultivate your patience with your team members, your manager, your project sponsor, your customer. In any case you need to take into account that you need always to work on the benefit of the project. I want to share with you some questions I recommend you in order to assess your patience:

1. How do you feel when your sponsor is not giving feedback to you?
2. How do you feel when your team member is not asking you any questions?
3. What is your feeling when your team has a problem that is very difficult to solve?
4. How do you feel when your customer is complaining you regarding a delay in a milestone or product delivery?

Chapter Summary

I would like to remind you some important ideas shared in this chapter about Passion, persistence and patience.

Passion

- I truly believe passion makes the difference between success and failure in our lives.
- Passion is very important. Following your passion is the secret to overcoming the setbacks all entrepreneurs face and it builds

resistance against the inevitable naysayers who will question your vision

- Passion is about believing in what you do, inspiring others to believe in it, and loving why you do what you do
- Passion requires courage, even young-like energy, to keep your eyes on your goal and do all you can to achieve it
- If you want to see enthusiasm as one of your goals, you also need to decide how you will measure it
- When you have the facts on which factors increase passion, and why, it is time to consider the obstacles standing in the way of inspiration

Persistence

- Being persistent is a skill that can help you to achieve a goal, get what you wish and can even be a means by which you assert yourself in the face of stubborn or difficult people
- The greater the achievement you seek, the more likely you will persist to achieve it
- Persistence is important in your life. It will mark how well you accomplish tasks that you set for yourself
- Those who persist end up with the health, fitness and vitality that we were striving for in the beginning when the motivation was high and the weather warm.

Patience

- Having patience means being able to wait calmly in the face of frustration or adversity, so anywhere there is frustration or adversity we have the opportunity to practice it
- Patience helps us achieve our goals, it is linked with good heath, patient people are better team members and colleagues
- Patience is connected to trust, hope, faith, love and good character

References

Bucero, A. 2010. *Today is a Good Day: Attitudes for Achieving Project Success.* Ontario, Canada: Multimedia Publications.

Englund, R.L., and A. Bucero. 2012. "The Complete Project Manager: Building the Right Set of Skills for Greater Project Success." Paper Presented at PMI® Global Congress 2012—EMEA, Marseille, France. Newtown Square, PA: Project Management Institute.

Mukwevho, A. 2013. *Burning Desire.* Grooming Man Human Development.

Mandino, O. 2007. *The Greatest Salesman in the World.* Jaico Publishing House.

Mischel, W., and Ebbesen, E.B. 1970. "Attention in Delay of Gratification." *Journal of Personality and Social Psychology*, 16(2), 329–337.

Vujicic, N. 2011. *Life Without Limits.* Australia and New Zealand: Allen & Unwin.

Young, S. 2016. *7 Must-Know Strategies to Learn Anything Faster.* E-book

Zak, P.J. May 19, 2009. *The Moral Molecule.* Gruter Institute Squaw Valley Conference 2009: Law, Behavior & the Brain. Available at SSRN: https://ssrn.com/abstract=1405393

CHAPTER 2

Developing Passion, Persistence, and Patience

Every great dream begins with a dreamer. Always remember, you have within you the strength, the patience, and the passion to reach for the stars to change the world.

—Harriet Tubman

As a leader, it is vital to immerse with passion and be passionate about what you do. Okay, I am not Mister Passionate the whole day, but I always focus my mindset every day on how I can be the best and use my passion to create change and greatness in others. In turn, somedays I have to do things I am not that passionate about, but I always focus on why I do what I do.

Also, I have worked with and met the most remarkable people: construction workers, technical specialists, sales assistants, team members, counselors, and people who you might think at times might not have the most fulfilling or exciting jobs, but they always find the purpose and passion around what they do.

In turn, if you are finding it difficult to be passionate or have passion in what you do, what do you need to change? Think about it. I met Ricardo Piscitelli, attorney and now Director of the Master in Project Management for Construction at QLU (Quality Leadership University) in Panama City. I have to say that he is doing an amazing work advising and supporting all the project management master's students through his passion for helping students to be successful. He is always ready to help and passionate about helping the students to find a professional future, understanding their needs and dreams better to give them the best orientation to their future. Our conversation centered around why do people change their lives when they are sick and are told devastating news. Please do not wait! Find passion in what you do, find your why—or change it!

How to Find Your Passion?

Life is short. If there was ever a moment to follow your passion and do something what matters to you, that moment is now. Figuring out what you are passionate about is a popular topic that finds its way into conversations with friends, at work, and in some books like this one. And it is a clear reminder that many of us will reach a point in our lives, if you haven't already, where the desire to leave behind the mundane to live a life you love is too strong to ignore. But trying to figure out exactly what you love to do can be challenging. We feel this intense urge to just "figure it out." But when we look around, that passion is nowhere to be found, and we aren't where we truly want to be. It frustrates us. It keeps us up at night. It makes us anxious as we notice more and more time is slipping away while we sit around feeling confused.

We see others who have seemingly identified their "thing," their passion, their calling, and we hope one day that we will get there too. While I don't feel like I'm remotely qualified to tell others how to live their lives by a long shot, I am the most qualified person to speak on my own life and share the things that I've found helpful in pushing me along my journey to figuring out what I'm most passionate about. I wanted to share with you seven suggestions to find your passion:

1. *Do many things.*

    I really cannot stress the importance of this one enough. Having lots of interests may feel overwhelming, but it is actually a great problem to have despite how much you feel you are "all over the place." When you are on the journey to figuring out what you love most, this is one of the most crucial steps and it is actually quite simple. Do things. Do a lot of things. It is better to have lots of options and interests than none at all. Make a list of all the things you are interested in, pick two to focus on first, and then get busy. Find some classes to see if these things are something you really want to pursue further. If you realize it is not what you thought it would be, scratch it off of your list and move on. If you end up loving it and find yourself consistently wanting to do more of it, then you are on to something.

2. *Always stay true to yourself.*

Just because your degree says you have fulfilled the requirements to go out and get a job in a certain industry doesn't mean you will always love doing that. You are entitled to change your mind whenever you want, and you can and should always follow the path where your heart leads. Where does that path lead? I believe it leads to true joy. We often try to place limits on ourselves after we've invested so much money in school and move into the working world: feeling stuck at jobs with horrible bosses, low pay, and in cities that just aren't what we expected. The secret to getting unstuck is not hard at all.

Stop doing what you hate and begin taking the steps to doing what you love. You do not have to feel confined to a box and you should not worry about being defined by one thing. As much as I love traveling, writing, and inspiring others through my own journey, I am also passionate about my mindfulness practice and healthy living. And I love sharing my wellness journey with others just as much as my travel plans. I embrace having multiple interests even if I'm not quite sure how I can combine them all into one perfect identity—and right now, I don't feel the need to.

3. *Focus on you.*

However, if you go about finding your passion, you definitely will not find it by watching and comparing where you are in life to others. If it seems as if your friends are further along in their career or like they have it all figured out, nine times out of 10 I can assure you they don't have it all figured out, no matter how many filters they use on those pictures. But, maybe they did take a big leap of faith, move across the country, or sacrifice relationships to get to where they are. Whatever it is, you cannot compare your journey to theirs.

4. *Let go of fear.*

Fear is the ultimate buzz kill. It can convince you to pass up some of the most amazing opportunities all because you cannot see past taking that first step. I don't know about you, but I don't like walking around in the dark. You don't know if you've got a clear path or if you're going to bang your knee on the coffee table. But in order to get to the other side of the room so that you can turn on the light, you just have to get through the hard part and the uncertainty. In order to find your passion, big leaps of faith are mandatory.

5. *Be still.*

As counterproductive as this one seems, we tend to get so confused at times with all of the thoughts, ideas, and emotions swarming through our minds that we get frustrated because we just cannot seem to figure it out. Time is passing by fast and according to our checklist, we were supposed to be knee-deep in our passion by age 25. The reality is, for some of us, this takes a bit longer than our expectations want to accept. Sometimes giving ourselves a moment of stillness to simply do nothing is just what we need to realize that what we are passionate about has been right in front of us the entire time.

6. *Forget about the money.*

A dollar, euro, or whatever currency amount should never be the determining factor of what you do in life and if it is, more than likely you will always end up in positions doing things you're not passionate about just to make a coin. When you are truly passionate about something, you do it because you genuinely love doing it first, and then you figure out how to make a living from it. I have been delivering many talks at professional conferences in project management for free just because I enjoyed, learned, and got fun.

7. *Know that everyone will not "get" you.*

If I have learned one thing throughout the past few years, it is to limit the amount of advice I solicit from people who are not qualified to offer their counsel on what I am doing with my life. Some people will never "get" you or your visions and that is okay. It's not for them to understand anyway. Spend less time explaining or rationalizing your goals and dreams and surround yourself with people who can propel you further while you are busy working toward discovering your passion.

There is a difference between two kinds of passion: harmonious and obsessive (Kaufman 2016). People with harmonious passion have the ability to disconnect when work is over, easily transitioning into their lives outside of the office. Obsessive people don't have that ability, and here's what that all amounts to.

A recent study investigated burnout (measured by emotional exhaustion) in two samples of nurses over a six-month period across two different countries. Obsessive passion increased the chances of burnout while harmonious passion helped protect against burnout. The researchers identified some key factors explaining this relationship. Obsessive passion was associated with higher conflict with other life tasks and was unrelated to work satisfaction, while harmonious passion was associated with lower conflict and higher work satisfaction. Importantly, these effects held even after controlling for the number of hours worked.

People with harmonious passion come to work refreshed and are ready to tackle new problems, whereas those with obsessive passion are at much higher risk of experiencing burnout. So, what do you do if you are obsessively passionate? Let go. That is easier said than done, of course, so taking an extreme approach might be necessary. Set times when you are simply not available and adhere to them. Make your computer inaccessible at certain hours of the day. You may have trouble adjusting at first, but you're headed for burnout if you don't force yourself to restrain your passion to healthy amounts. You may love your job, but it's important to love other things as well. The more you come to appreciate things outside of work, the easier it will be to let obsession subside.

How to Develop Your Passion?

Maybe you struggle to feel passion around others, or to feel passionate as an individual. Developing passion is part of an active process to become a more compelling and emotional person and requires a proactive approach to living. You can develop a more passionate attitude by doing fun and exciting things, focusing on creativity and using your imagination, and by interacting passionately with others. I have some suggestions for you, according to the Figure 2.1 as follows:

1. *Think about your childhood hopes and dreams.*
   If you are struggling to identify your passion, you may want to consider what you enjoyed doing as a child. Make a list of the activities you lived for as a kid, from playing with Legos to dressing up dolls. Consider if you would enjoy doing that activity now but in

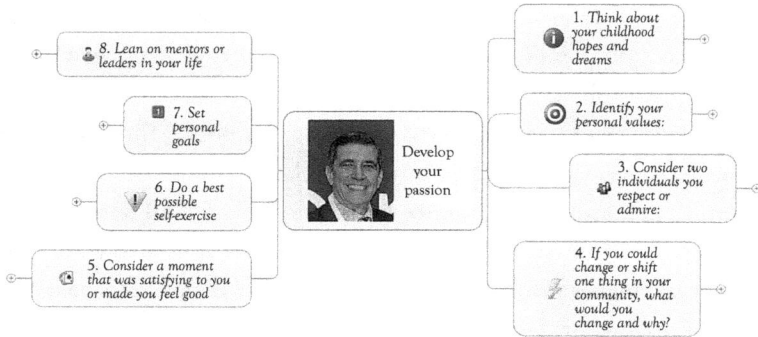

Figure 2.1 Develop your passion

a different context. If you were really into building with Legos, for example, this could indicate your passions might lie in architecture or construction. If you enjoyed dressing up your dolls, this could indicate your passions might be geared more toward fashion or styling. Taking a childhood passion and translating it into a viable job or field of study could lead to a more fulfilling career and a fuller life. In my personal case I enjoyed reading books and novels, swimming and teaching others to swim.

2. *Identify your personal values.*

   Your personal values are your core principal beliefs or the ideas that are the most important to you. Determining your personal values can help you determine if you are passionate about your job, your field of study, or even your relationships. You can ask yourself some guiding questions to help identify your personal values. For example:

   • Do you believe in your job?

   • Do you enjoy your job and everyday cannot wait to go for work because you love it?

   • Do you like people, talking, discussing, and arguing among them?

3. *Consider two individuals you respect or admire.*

   • Why do you admire them?

   • What characteristics do they embody that you admire or appreciate?

4. *If you could change or shift one thing in your community, what would you change and why?*
   - What world issue would you change if you could?
   - What issues or problem get you the most charged in conversation with others?

5. *Consider a moment that was satisfying to you or made you feel good:* Identify that moment and consider why you felt so satisfied in that moment. Look over your answers to these questions and try to identify any themes or common ideas. These principles, beliefs, and ideas are likely some of your personal values. You can then use your personal values to help you determine your priorities in life and how these priorities can shape your passions in your career, your schooling, and your relationships.

6. *Do a best possible self-exercise.*
   Your "best possible future self" is a personalized representation of your goals and the future you envision for yourself. Doing a best possible self-exercise can help you gain better insight into your goals, priorities, and motivations. It can also help you to gain some control of your trajectory in school or in a career using critical thinking and self-analysis. To do the exercise, use this prompt: "Consider your life in the future. Imagine that everything in your life has gone as well as it possibly could. You have managed to achieve all your life goals. You have realized your life dreams. Now, write down what you imagine." Write to this prompt for 20 minutes a day for three days. On the fourth day, read over your responses. Highlight or circle any repeating themes, ideas, goals, or aspirations. These could be a good indication of where your passions lie and how you can pursue them.

7. *Set personal goals.*
   Another way to home in on your passions is to set personal goals. This can motivate you to pursue a certain passion that could then turn into a career option or an educational option. Writing down your personal goals requires you to be self-reflective and consider what is meaningful to you. It also requires you prioritize and narrow down your ideas to form clear personal goals. Once you have formed your personal goals, you should create a schedule to determine

when you will need to achieve these goals. You may have different timeframes for different personal goals, depending on how simple or complex they are.

Creating personal goals will also allow you to identify what you are already doing in your daily routine to achieve certain goals and what are the skills you need to learn or develop to achieve certain goals. This can be highly motivating and a very active way to determine your passion in life.

8. *Lean on mentors or leaders in your life.*

If you are struggling to identify your passion and goals, you may want to reach out to a mentor or leader in your life who can offer advice or guidance. This could be a teacher, parent, community member, or even a sibling or friend. Have a discussion with this mentor about possible career paths you are interested in and how you can access this path. Sit down with your mentor and talk about your personal values and goals and how you can translate these into a viable career or field of study. Often, mentors whom you are close with can give you some perspective on your options and encourage you to pursue goals or passions that you enjoy and may excel at.

Are You Persistent?

Talent, genius, and education mean very little when persistence is lacking. Here's what true determination looks like. In any discussion of the attributes of successful people, persistence is always mentioned often as the, or one of the, most important factors in success. As a project manager, major success seldom comes easily or without a great deal of effort. Often the only difference between those who succeed and those who don't is the ability to keep going long after the rest have dropped out. It's relatively easy to persist when things are going well and we see progress, but highly persistent people have found ways to keep going despite major setbacks and a lack of evidence that they are moving closer toward their goals. Here are some of the things that persistent people have in common that keeps them going long after most people have given up:

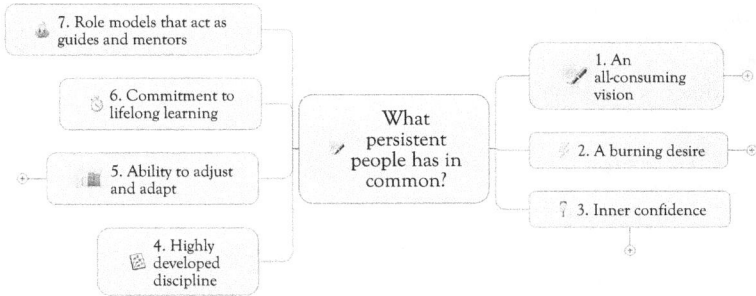

Figure 2.2 What persistent people have in common

According to Figure 2.2, I will explain what persistent people have in common:

1. *An all-consuming vision*

   Persistent people have a goal or vision in mind that motivates and drives them (Blanchard and Hersey 1993). They are often dreamers and visionaries who see their lives as having a higher purpose than simply earning a living. Their vision is deeply ingrained, and they focus on it constantly and with great emotion and energy. They often think of this vision first thing when they wake up and last thing before they go to bed. Reaching this goal becomes the focal point of their life and they devote a major portion of their energies and time toward reaching it.

2. *A burning desire*

   As an entrepreneur and motivational speaker, I always say, "If you really want to do something, you will find a way. If you don't, you will find an excuse." Persistent people want it bad, really bad, and they never look for an excuse or a way out. What keeps highly persistent people going is their powerful level of desire. Repeated failures, dead ends, and periods when it seems like no progress is being made often come before any major breakthroughs happen. Persistent people have the inner energy and intensity to keep them motivated and going through these tough times.

3. *Inner confidence*

People who overcome the odds and achieve greatly are often described as "marching to the beat of their own drummer."[1] They know what they want and are seldom swayed by the opinion of the masses. Having a highly developed sense of who they are allows the highly persistent to continue on without being greatly affected by what others think of them or, being understood, or being appreciated by those around them. While that inner confidence gets challenged and shaken, it never gets destroyed and constantly acts as a source of courage and determination.

4. *Highly developed discipline*

Motivation is what helps you to start. Discipline is what keeps you going. Highly persistent people know it is very difficult to stay continually motivated, particularly during difficult times and when it appears that no progress is being made. They have come to rely upon their self-discipline and developing habits they can count on to continue down the path toward their eventual goals. They believe the results of the efforts they make today may not be seen for a long time, but they strongly believe that everything they do will count toward their outcome in the end.

5. *Ability to adjust and adapt*

Persistent people have the ability to adjust and adapt their action plan. They do not stubbornly persist in the face of evidence that their plan is not working but look for better ways that will increase their chances of success. The highly persistent see their journey as a series of dead ends, detours, and adjustments but have complete faith they will reach their final destination. They are not tied into their ego and are quickly willing to admit when something is not working. As well, they are quick to adapt the ideas of others that have been shown to work well.

6. *Commitment to lifelong learning*

Persistent people realize that any goal worth reaching will take time, effort, and continuously learning new skills and thinking patterns.

---

[1] If people march to the beat of their own drum, they do things the way they want without taking other people into consideration.

They welcome change and new ideas and continue looking for ways they can incorporate these into their lives. Ongoing learning is seen as part of a process through which the highly persistent continually expand the range of tools that they have to work with. Naturally curious, persistent types not only see learning as a way to reach their goals more quickly, but they also see self-development as a way of life. Learning and continual growth do not end at a certain age or stage of life, but they are the essence of life itself, and therefore never-ending.

7. *Role models who act as guides and mentors*

While it may appear that highly persistent people act alone and don't need anyone, most have a carefully chosen group of people they admire and emulate. These can be people who are actually involved in their lives as mentors or confidantes or they can be figures who they have read about and who have deeply impacted them. You will know who these people are since persistent people will often quote them.

Persistent people usually stand out from their environment and are often misunderstood or ridiculed because they can make those around them feel uncomfortable. Having strongly ingrained models helps persistent people sustain and motivate themselves in an environment that is not always supportive.

Develop Your Persistence

I strongly believe that persistence is a "muscle" you need to exercise as a project manager to achieve your goals. Here are my three top tips for building your persistence muscle.

1. *Focus on the outcome.* Get clear on what you are working toward and why it is worth pursuing. If something is important enough to you, then you will find a way. Visualize completing the project, task, or overcoming the challenge and notice how you will feel when it is done. For example, I am doing that when writing a book and this one is my number 10.

2. *Develop your belief.* More than anything, persistence is about belief—belief in you! Without belief that you are good enough, smart enough or worthy enough it is so often too tempting to give up when things get hard, boring, challenging, or painful. Your belief in yourself and in the goals, you are going after will help you to continue. Repeat in front of the mirror every day that you are excellent. After 20 days that thought will be part of your mindset, so you need to make some adjustments to be excellent because if not you will see the same like Pinocchio (getting your nose growing because you lied).

3. *Enlist support.* Doing it alone is doing it the hard way. Reach out, collaborate, or ask for help or support. If you do not have belief in you yet, enlist a colleague, coach, or mentor who believes in you to lift you up, push you on, and hold you accountable. If you do not have a mentor yet, please find one because it is worth for you as a great professional.

When I first started out in my own business, I had a dream and big goals. But I was afraid and uncertain. I didn't have 100 percent belief that I had what it took to create a successful business, so I found a mentor who I believed in and who believed in me. When my belief wavered, my mentor propped me up, provided encouragement, and gave me the tools to make persisting so much easier.

To persist at anything is a choice. At any time, we can choose to keep going, keep fighting, keep learning, and keep finding ways to achieve or we can choose to give up, say that we tried but failed or simply move onto something else that seems easier or more fun. But I know that if we want to play a bigger game, achieve new goals, and progress our careers so as we really make a difference, then persistence is required. Giving up or taking the easy road is not an option.

And remember, there are no overnight success stories. Success in any area of our life takes persistence and hard work. And without it you are only dreaming. Remember, persistence is a choice.

Cultivate Your Patience

As virtues go, patience is a quiet one. It's often exhibited behind closed doors, not on a public stage: a father telling a third bedtime story to his son and a dancer waiting for her injury to heal. In public, it's the impatient ones who grab all our attention: drivers honking in traffic, grumbling customers in slow-moving lines. We have epic movies exalting the virtues of courage and compassion but a movie about patience might be a bit of a snoozer.

Yet patience is essential to daily life and might be key to a happy one. Having patience means being able to wait calmly in the face of frustration or adversity, so anywhere there is frustration or adversity—that is, nearly everywhere—we have the opportunity to practice it. At home with our kids, at work with our colleagues, at the grocery store with half our city's population, patience can make the difference between annoyance and equanimity, between worry and tranquility. Religions and philosophers have long praised the virtue of patience; now researchers are starting to do so as well.

All of us as project managers have the opportunity to manage the organization. We need to preach the organization about the characteristics, benefits, and advantages of the project-based organization and how by practicing the project management discipline our organization will achieve better and better results.

Recent studies have found that, sure enough, good things really do come to those who wait (Dolan 2010). This is all good news for the naturally patient—or for those who have the time and opportunity to take an intensive two-week training in patience. But what about the rest of us? It seems there are everyday ways to build patience as well. Here are some strategies suggested by emerging patience research.

- *Reframe the situation.* Feeling impatient is not just an automatic emotional response; it involves conscious thoughts and beliefs, too. If a colleague is late to a meeting, you can fume about their lack of respect, or see those extra 15 minutes as an opportunity to get some reading done. Patience is linked to self-control and consciously trying to regulate our emotions can help us train our self-control muscles.
- *Practice mindfulness.* In one study, kids who did a six-month mindfulness program in school became less impulsive and more willing to wait for a reward. I recommend mindfulness practice for project managers: Taking a deep breath and

noticing your feelings of anger or overwhelm (for example, when your team members start yet another argument because they did not achieve their deliverable deadline) can help you respond with more patience.

- *Practice gratitude.* In another study, adults who were feeling grateful were also better at patiently delaying gratification. When given the choice between getting an immediate cash reward or waiting a year for a larger ($100) windfall, less grateful people caved in once the immediate payment offer climbed to $18. Grateful people, however, could hold out until the amount reached $30. If we're thankful for what we have today, we're not desperate for more stuff or better circumstances immediately.

We can try to shelter ourselves from frustration and adversity, but they come with the territory of being human. Practicing patience in everyday situations—like with our punctuality-challenged coworker—will not only make life more pleasant in the present but might also help pave the way for a more satisfying and successful future.

I will share with you some best practices to develop your patience.

- *Divide it by time.* Tackle a task in 15 or 30 minutes or one-hour pieces. If you are trying to change your habits, go for one day and then another. If you want to write, tackle half a page at a time.
- *Use the same approach to complete any new habit.* Start a side project with the same mindset and you will stay persistent. Spend a few minutes on your life's work after work every day.
- *Three times per week is better than nothing,* and it might not seem so difficult. Then, build it up from there.
- *Learn what motivates you and ride on that.* Use motivation to your advantage. Challenge yourself to finish a certain amount or to get through a certain amount of time.
- *Keep score.* Write your progress in a journal or calendar. Progress is the ultimate motivator. Once you see results, you will strive to continue.

- *Reward yourself for persisting.* Big goals can take months or even years to achieve. The longer the time it takes to achieve the goal, the more you risk losing motivation. Reward small actions toward bigger goals. That way you are more likely to persist with reaching your bigger goal.

Greatness is not measured by what is accomplished. It is measured by how many times you pick yourself up and try.

Summary and Conclusions

In this chapter I have been sharing my experiences, thoughts, and ideas about how to develop passion, persistence, and patience. Some lessons learned are as follows:

- As a leader, it is vital to turn up with passion and be passionate about what you do.
- But trying to figure out exactly what you love to do can be challenging.
- People with harmonious passion come to work refreshed and ready to tackle new problems, whereas those with obsessive passion are at much higher risk of experiencing burnout.
- Developing passion is part of an active process to become a more compelling and emotional person and requires a proactive approach to living.
- Try to find your passion doing many things, being focused on you, staying true to yourself, letting go of fear, being still, forgetting about the money, and taking into account that not everyone will respond, work, or act at your pace.
- Developing passion is part of an active process to become a more compelling and emotional person and requires a proactive approach to living.
- Focus on the outcome, develop your belief, and enlist support.
- Some best practices to develop your patience: divide it by time, use the same approach to complete any new habit,

three times per week is better than nothing, learn what motivates you and ride on that, keep score, and reward yourself for persisting. Now it is your time, you have read the description about how to develop your passion, persistence and patience. Take action and prepare your 3ps development plan, and set some milestones your achievements.

References

Blanchard, K.H., and P. Hersey. 1993. *Management of Organizational Behaviour.* New Jersey: Prentice Hall.

Dolan, G. 2010. *Ignite: Real Leadership, Real Talk, Real Results.* Wiley.

Kaufman, S.B., and C. Gregoire. 2016. *Wired to Create: Unraveling the Mysteries of the Creative Mind.* Random House.

CHAPTER 3

Sustaining My 3Ps

Passion is energy.
Feel the power that comes from focusing on what excites you.
—Oprah Winfrey

It is quite easy to announce and share what is your principle, but it is quite difficult to sustain it, not impossible. Project management is my passion so I always try to feed up my passion in all the projects and initiatives I lead and I am engaged or dreaming about positive outcomes. In order to convert those projects into a reality, I need to be persistent because sometimes I may fail, and I need to cultivate my patience because all those efforts take time and dedication. In order to sustain my 3Ps, I need to be disciplined because daily facts and our environment are usually toxic, I mean, create or generate some obstacles to sustain your passion, persistence, and patience.

Some Stories to Share

Let me share with you the story of my career as a book author. Writing a book is a very challenging project because you need to transmit what you lived in a way in which your audience is able to understand, so you need to be careful about "how to express it." My story is as follows: I always enjoyed writing summaries since I was a child. When I was hired by Fujitsu Spain as my first job I worked as a product support engineer for an American product and at the same time I was finishing my engineering degree. I took advantage of my job activities to write my final degree assignment. I dedicated a lot of time on a daily basis to write and edit it. I learned a lot from my mentor that time.

Then I moved to DEC (Digital Equipment Corporation) in Spain (Madrid office) and I started writing about software development and project management basics. I submitted my first article to a Spanish technical magazine and after some feedback and corrections from that magazine editors, my article was accepted and published. I received some comments from a colleague about if I copied the article from someone else. It was the first time I found a "dream killer." Instead of demotivating me, that comment encouraged me to move forward. Every two or three months I submitted an article to that magazine and I learned a lot about how to be more concise writing an article.

Some years later I moved to Hewlett Packard in Spain, and I was responsible for the project management initiative there, so I took the initiative of writing a monthly newsletter to spread out the project management knowledge in that organization. I only wrote one page. I made a special effort of compiling my thoughts, ideas, and message in only one page, because people had not enough time to read more than one page. That initiative gave me the opportunity to read and research more, and also to learn how to address and customize my newsletters to my audience. Initially my target audience were project managers and managers from my department. Writing those newsletters monthly, after four years I had 48 newsletters written on different project management subjects. So, I thought why not to write a book? Then I decided to write it. I had a lot of material from my newsletters, I had managed many projects over the years, and I had researched about theory and definitions in the project management field.

I was blessed. I had all the ingredients to move forward. What I needed was first of all to have some time to compose my book and then to get an executive sponsoring that project. That time I was responsible for the Project Management Office (PMO) in my organization. That office was operating quite reasonably, but the management did not believe in project management, so I discovered that I would not be supported internally at all. Thanks to be responsible for the PMO, I had to travel worldwide so frequently and attended several conferences and congresses where I presented some papers. That situation allowed me to create a contacts network worldwide. That year I met one lady in one of the conferences outside Spain, and she gave me the idea of starting up a project management services company in Spain. One Mexican colleague contacted me, so I travelled to Mexico City and I decided to leave the company I worked for and create mine, and I did it at the beginning of 2002. In the meanwhile, I was writing my book and advancing during nights on the edits. Three months later I got an agreement with a multinational company in the United States (New York) and one of the parts of my agreement was to get my book published.

Then I moved forward and started my own company's operations representing the services from the American company in Spain. My book was published six months later by "Lito Grapo" editors in Mexico DF (now called Mexico City). It was a well-received book because that time there were not much literature published in Spanish language on project management.

In that real story I maintained my passion over those years because I love my profession and I believe in that I was persistent writing for a while every day after hours during almost one year, and I used my patience to find my right sponsor to get my book published. A big part of your success comes from how you are able to maintain and sustain your passion, persistence, and patience.

From 2002 to 2004, I was representing an American company in Spain, but the financial crisis set in during 2003 so I needed to travel continuously outside Spain. I travelled to Mexico, France, Germany, Russia, Denmark, and several countries week after week. At the same time, I tried to manage my Spanish company and it was a continuous nightmare. My project management passion was still there but it was so stressful, time demanding, and I could stay with my family during many weekends. Then I made the decision of leaving the American company and continuing in my own. It was a difficult decision because I would not have the support from that US company anymore. In fact, I would be alone in front of the market again.

It took me close to one month to analyze the benefits and advantages that I would get letting go of the US company and moving forward on my own. I needed to use my patience here, because even when I left my US company and restarted mine, I was managing my old company and the new one at the same time. My US partner did not find a managing director for the Spanish office and I agreed to help them for a while. Then, I was applying my passion to move forward with my own company and strategy. My passion helped me to make the effort managing two companies at the same time for a four-month period. It was very heavy for my mind and body, and I needed to be persistent finding new customers for my own company because I was constrained on time and movements. But again, the application of my 3Ps (passion, persistence, and patience) were really helpful to overcome those obstacles.

Some Best Practices

The application of persistence to any task, interaction, or goal is often what distinguishes between those who are successful and those who fail in any endeavor. Indeed, a lack of persistence or "giving up too soon" is one of the most common reasons for failure in any endeavor.

We are complex creatures. I believe that hope and anguish can coexist and still create something truly amazing. Persistence is the ability to maintain action regardless of your feelings (Pavlina 2009). You press on even when you feel like quitting, until you achieve that important goal. I surprise myself every day. People give up too soon because they have wrong expectations of themselves and the outcome. They expect the way to be easy, and they are surprised when they find the reality to be the opposite. Their enthusiasm quickly melts and they lose heart. So, start your journey with the right expectation. And don't underestimate the amount of time required either.

Everyone says they are doing something because they love it. My observation is that it is easier to love something when you are winning. I define my professional passion by three attributes that I consider as best practices: *commitment to domain, questing, and connecting* (Figure 3.1). Each of these attributes leads to behaviors that drive sustained performance improvement and help people integrate knowledge from professional networks and lessons from difficult challenges into a disciplined commitment toward making an increasing longer-term impact.

Commitment to domain: Long-term commitment can be understood as a desire to have a lasting and increasing impact on a particular domain and a desire to participate in that domain for the foreseeable future. Commitment to domain helps individuals focus on where they can make the most impact. Having domain context enables an individual to learn much

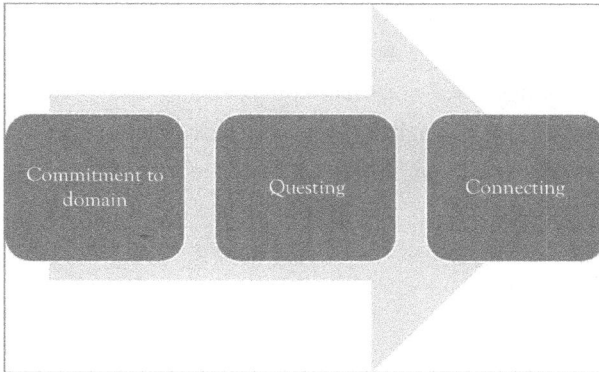

Figure 3.1 Three attributes of passion as best practices

faster, allowing for cumulative learning. This commitment, however, does not imply isolation or tunnel vision. Quite the opposite: These individuals are constantly seeking lessons and innovative practices from adjacent and new domains that have the potential to influence their chosen domain.

Commitment to domain is important because it can carry an individual through the inevitable bumps and disappointments that come, even in good work environments, over the course of a career. For example, I am committed to my project management profession. I am a project manager practitioner over the years. I discovered I like writing and speaking in public too. Then I was exploring how to write and how to speak in public better and better. It took me some time and effort, but I am progressing on that purpose.

Questing: The questing disposition drives workers to go above and beyond their core responsibilities. Project managers with the questing disposition constantly probe, test, and push boundaries to identify new opportunities and learn new skills. Resourceful and imaginative, they experiment with novel ways of using the available tools and resources to improve their performance.

These project managers actively seek challenges that might help them achieve the next level of performance. If they cannot find the types of challenges that generate learning, individuals with a questing disposition are likely to become frustrated and move to another environment (such as a new team or organization) that does offer these opportunities. During my career I always tried to take some risk and apply my courage trying to do some things I was not totally prepared for. One example was my first talk in front of an English audience. To do that I was practicing and rehearsing my presentation in English for three months. I was not totally successful, but my audience congratulated me on my effort. Even when my delivery was not perfect, but it encouraged me to deliver public talks again and again to progress.

Connecting: The connecting disposition leads individuals to seek out others to help find solutions to the challenges they are facing. Although networking—connecting with and learning from others—is commonly understood as an effective way to advance, those with a connecting disposition seek deep interactions with others in related domains to attain insights that they can bring back into their own domain. Workers driven by a connecting disposition build connection, not to grow their professional networks but to learn from experts and build new knowledge and capabilities. My suggestion learned from experience is that you need to build up your network connections and maintain it. Put your focus on that and you will be more successful, but the key is not just connected but maintain your connections.

Project managers who exhibit all three attributes have what we have defined as the passion of the explorer. Because of their potential for dramatic impact in their organizations, management needs to get better at recognizing and cultivating passion in the workforce to transform their businesses. Passionate workers will thrive in the right work environment, and workers with some, but not all, of the attributes are key targets for internal talent development efforts to increase this limited stock of resilient workers.

Some Food for Your Mind

What is the meaning of "some food for your mind"? Every mind is lazy as a principle. Our brain is another muscle of your body. We are used to exercise the physical muscles but not as much the brain muscles. Are you familiar with mindfulness?

There are a couple of definitions about that:

- The quality or state of being conscious or aware of something[1]
- A mental state achieved by focusing one's awareness on the present moment, while calmly acknowledging and accepting one's feelings, thoughts, and bodily sensations, used as a therapeutic technique[2]

Recently received a call from a friend who wanted to know if I still loved my job with the same passion that I had for it when I first started working as a project manager. My answer was: A job is like a love affair; when you find one that you love passionately, you feel very strongly about it at first. You cannot wait to get to work and you do not mind spending most of your time on it. But as time goes by, your passion may be tempered. It does not go away altogether; you only replace it with affection, persistence, and patience. Any relationship is similar—you do not have the same passion that you did when starting out, but you do share a solid bond that is built on love, trust, and togetherness.

The key to sustaining passion for your job as a project manager is the same as maintaining it in a relationship—you need to work at it (Figure 3.2). And to do this, you need to:

- *Focus on what you love about it*: Just like you would focus on the positives of your relationship with your spouse or significant other to make it work and sustain your interest in each other, so too must you think more about the good aspects of your job in order to continue to do it with the same amount of passion and interest that you initially had for it.
- *Think of the benefits you achieve*: When you think about the good salary you're being paid, the convenient work timings, your friendly colleagues and all the other aspects of your job

[1] Consciousness | Definition of Consciousness by Merriam-Webster
https://merriam-webster.com/dictionary/consciousness
[2] Mindfulness | Definition of mindfulness in English by Oxford Dictionaries
https://en.oxforddictionaries.com/definition/mindfulness

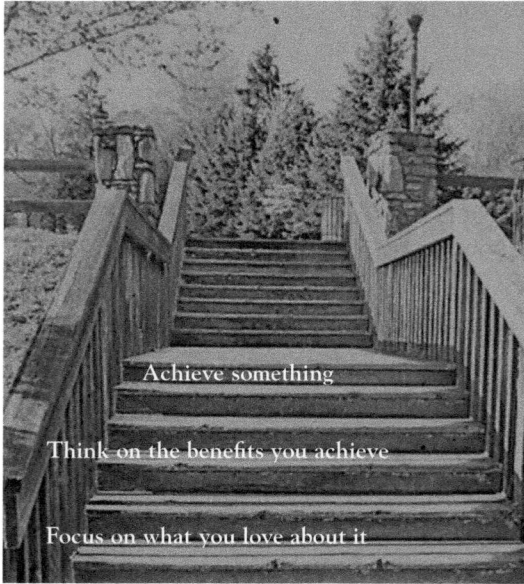

Figure 3.2 Sustaining passion

that people consider advantages, you tend to feel better about
it even though you do not have the same passionate attitude
about it as you originally did.
* *Achieve something*: When you are able to achieve significant
successes on the job, when your work continues to bring in
praise and acclaim, and when you know that you are making
a positive difference to your organization, it's easy to smile on
the job and be passionate about it every day.

It is important that you continue to love your job, because the minute
you lose interest, you become less efficient and start making mistakes,
which could turn out to be costly in more ways than one. So please work
on sustaining your passion for what you do, and watch work turn out to
be much more than just a job.

Suggested Exercises to Do

We cannot force people to become passionate. A team leader needs to
create the right conditions for passion to emerge. Those conditions need

to be nurtured or tended to, not unlike a gardener creating the right conditions for his plants to flourish.

Let's reflect about it. Gardeners do not make plants grow—the genetic coding inside each plant does that. A gardener simply creates conditions that are conducive to plant growth. If those conditions are maintained then growth happens. A conscientious gardener frequently evaluates of the garden. Is fertilizer needed? Does the garden need more or less water? Are there any unwanted pesticides or diseases?

I suggest you to practice five exercises in order to cultivate and sustain your passion:

Exercise 1: Revisit your childhood (Figure 3.3)

- What did you love to do? It is amazing how disconnected we become to the things that brought us the most joy in favor of what is practical.
- Can you remember how did you enjoy when you were a child?
- Did you play alone or with some friends?
- Did you enjoy the adventures or did you prefer the quietness?

Those type of questions need to be answered to help you understanding what you really loved those times. Try to practice this exercise several times.

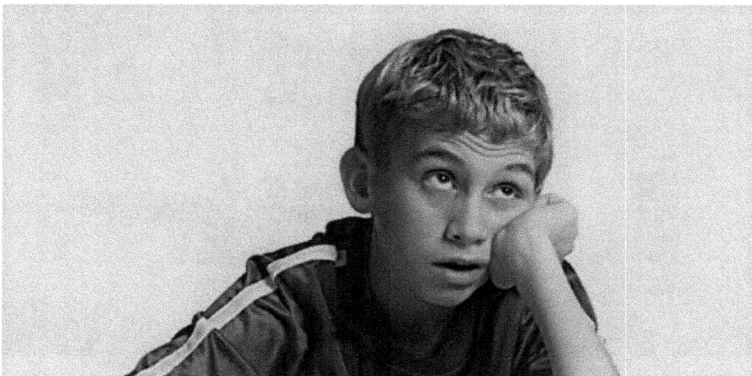

Figure 3.3 Revisit your childhood

Exercise 2: Make a creativity board (Figure 3.4)

Start by preparing a large poster board, and post the words you like in the center and create a collage of images, sayings, articles, poems, and other inspirations. The idea behind of that is that when you surround yourself with images of your intention—who you want to become or what you want to create—your awareness and passion will grow.

Images are powerful reminders of the things or actions we enjoyed and made feel us happier.

Exercise 3: Make a list of people who are where you want to be (Figure 3.5)

Study people who have been successful in the area you want to pursue. Study them, figure out how and why they are able to remain successful when everyone else is folding and then set up structures to emulate them. It will take you some time, but it is worth.

Exercise 4: Start doing what you love, even without a business (Figure 3.6)

Do what you enjoy, even if you have not yet figured out to monetize it. Invest time and effort working on that. For instance, I like public speaking and I am focused on improving my skills to do that day after day. I am always looking for opportunities to speak on public even as a volunteer sometimes.

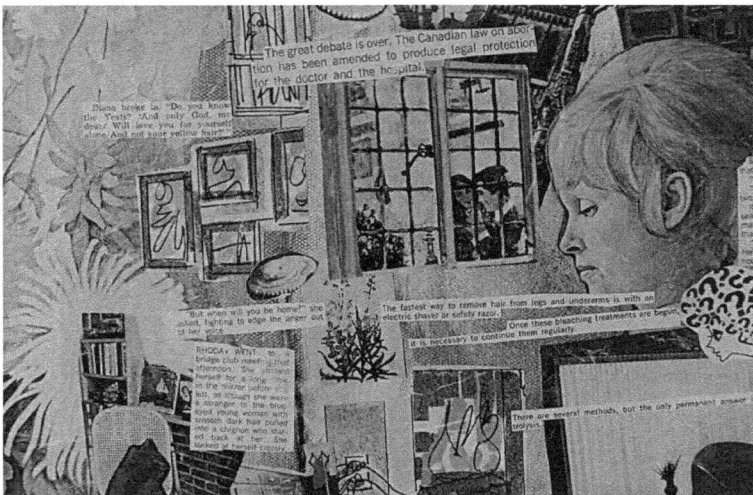

Figure 3.4 Make a creativity board

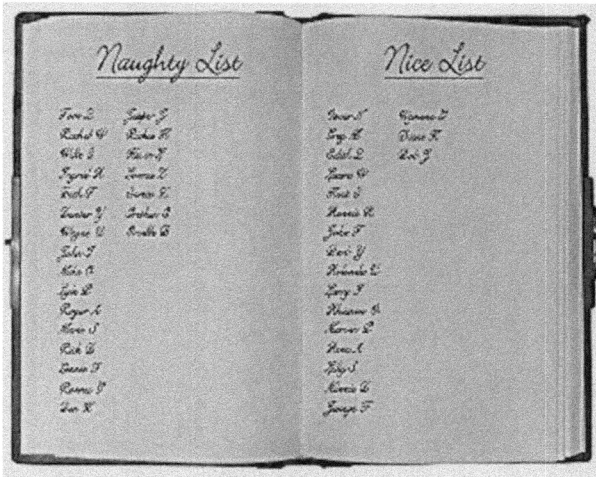

Figure 3.5 List of people who are where you want to be

Figure 3.6 Do what you love

Exercise 5: Take a break from business thinking (Figure 3.7)
While it might feel uncomfortable to step outside of business mode, the mind sometimes needs a rest from such bottom-line thinking. Rest for a while and you will return with some more energy and fresh ideas. From time to time everybody needs some time off. Sometimes professionals are obsessed about not decrease their productivity, but you need some rest from time to time to recharge your batteries.

Figure 3.7 Take a break

Chapter Summary

From the ideas, experiences and suggestions shared in this chapter, I would like to remark some of them:

- It is quite easy to announce and share what is your principle. It is quite difficult to sustain it, not impossible.
- The application of my 3Ps (passion, persistence, and patience) were really helpful to overcome those obstacles.
- The key, psychologists say, may lie in the difference between two mindsets: harmonious passion and obsessive passion.
- I define my professional passion by three attributes that I consider best practices: *commitment to domain, questing,* and *connecting.*
- The key to sustaining passion for your job is the same as maintaining it in a relationship—you must work at it.
- A team leader needs to create the right conditions for passion to emerge. Those conditions need to be nurtured or tended to, not unlike a gardener creating the right conditions for his plants to flourish.

Reference

Pavlina, S. 2009. *Personal Development for Smart People: The Conscious Pursuit of Personal Growth.*

CHAPTER 4

Be Contagious

Be a contagious mosquito all the time and infect your organization positively.

—Alfonso Bucero

A big part of your success comes from how you are able to maintain and sustain your passion, persistence, and patience. You need to dedicate time to do it, and in this chapter, I will share with you what I learned about sustaining my 3Ps. Not all the project managers have a positive behavior all the time. I learned over the years that every project manager needs to spend some time trying to be more positive when dealing with team members, customers, and other stakeholders. Some people confuse mood with attitude. A project manager can be in a good mood or in a bad mood every day, but his attitude needs to be positive the maximum amount of time. If you believe, you can infect your colleagues, peers, bosses, and other project stakeholders positively in organizations.

The Virus of Positive Attitude

I have found several definitions of a virus like *"an infective agent that typically consists of a nucleic acid molecule in a protein coat, is too small to be seen by light microscopy, and is able to multiply only within the living cells of a host"* or *"a harmful or corrupting influence"* (McConnell 2013). If we turn it around to a positive definition is what I am talking about. Be contagious as a positive mosquito in your project team, your organization, and your environment, and you will generate a more and more positive atmosphere. I have used that philosophy when helping organizations to implement a Project Management Office, project management methodologies, and implementing project portfolio management process.

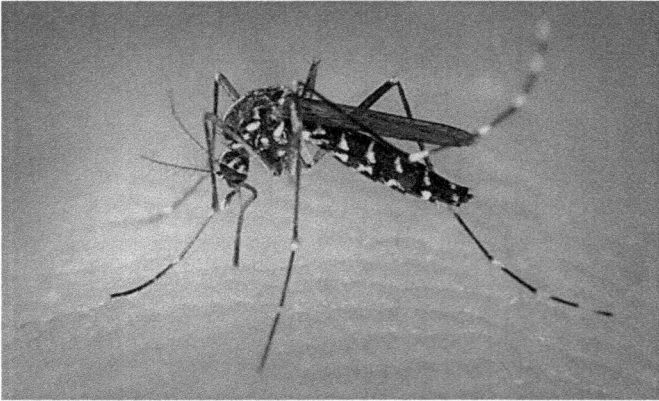

Figure 4.1 Be a positive infectious mosquito

Infection needs to be smooth but continuous (Figure 4.1). That way the virus of positivism will demonstrate that you achieve small but tangible results over time. You also need to feed up the virus looking for allies in your organization who are able to disseminate that virus more and more using passion, persistence, and patience.

Only through persistence you can achieve everything in your project management career. Alexander Graham Bell said, "What is power is I cannot say; all I know is that it exists and it becomes available only when a man is in that state of mind in which he knows exactly what he wants and is fully determined not to quit until he finds it." Persistence and patience are very interrelated, and both imply time and effort. In my experience every project professional must cultivate and develop persistence and transmit enthusiasm and positivism to his or her team. I have failed many times in my professional life, but I was willing to keep failing until I succeeded.

Projects are done by human beings who make right and wrong decisions during the project life cycle. This is part of human behavior that many executives forget during project execution in organizations. How to learn from successes and failures characterizes a project learning organization. One of the obligations from executives is to plan with their project managers for doing retrospective analysis during the project life cycle for each project. If lessons learned sessions are not planned as part of the project plan, they never will happen.

Trying hard and making many attempts is known as commitment and persistence in a general sense. Considering that projects are uncertain endeavors, project teams and project managers achieve right or wrong results. Depending on the point of view of those teams and leaders, the results will be considered as failures or as opportunities to learn. The learning attitude is a good characteristic of the right project leader. Every day I can learn something in my project, and it does not matter if I learn from my people, customer, or other project stakeholders. Good ideas or feedback can come from anywhere. The most important thing is how to move from failures to project success.

I can remember when I was a child, I learned how to ride a bicycle. Perhaps you had a similar experience that began with training wheels. Eventually, when these crutches were removed, keeping your balance became more difficult. You struggled to stay upright, maybe even falling a few times and scraping yourself. You were learning an important early lesson about failure. As you practiced, it is likely that one of your parents walked beside you shouting instructions, encouraging you and catching you as you lost balance. You were scared but excited. You looked forward to the time when you would succeed—when you would at last ride free on your own (Figure 4.2).

Figure 4.2 Try it again, and again

Or maybe you didn't think at all but were so wrapped up in the experience and how to accomplish the activity. Nobody called you a failure nor were you worried about failing. Then, you kept at it every day, and eventually mastered the skill of riding a bike. What contributed to your ultimate success in learning how to ride your bike?

Well, persistence and sheer repetition, certainly. You were going to stick with it no matter how long it took. It also helped that you were enthusiastic about what you set out to achieve that you could hardly wait to reach your goal. And finally, let's not underestimate the impact of positive encouragement. You always knew your parents were in your corner, supporting you and rooting for your success. As a youngster learning to ride your bike, you were optimistic, thrilled, and eager to meet the challenge. You could not wait to try again. You knew you would master it eventually. But that was a long time ago.

Yesterday and today: Now let's examine how most adults approach the development of new skills. Let's assume we asked a group of adults to learn a new software program or to switch to another position in the company. How would most respond? They would try to avoid it, they would complain, they would make excuses why they should not have to do it, they would doubt their abilities, and they would be afraid.

As adults, most of us become a lot more concerned about the opinions of others, often hesitating because people may laugh at us or criticize us. As a youngster, we knew we had to fall off the bike and get back on to learn a new skill. Falling off the bike was not a "bad" thing. But as we got older, we started to perceive falling off as a bad thing, rather than an essential part of the process of achieving our goal. It can be uncomfortable to try something new, perhaps even scary. But if you take your eyes off the goal and instead focus your attention on how others may be viewing you, you are doing yourself a grave disservice. To develop a new skill or reach a meaningful target, you must be committed to doing what it takes to get there, even if it means putting up with negative feedback or falling on your face now and then.

Successful people have learned to "fail" their way to success. While they may not particularly enjoy their "failures," they recognize them as a necessary part of the road to victory. Agile for instance advocates the same idea. Agile approaches to projects have been touted by more and more organizations across the globe. IT companies, frustrated over expensive projects falling well shy of their goals, have been desperate for change.

Within an Agile framework, there is a concept of failing fast and then recovering to move on to success. But in far too many organizations, failure is a concept that must never be uttered. Before Agile, failing projects had management standing up for them, explaining to users that the user community did not understand what was being asked of IT and that the insufficient solution was what users, obviously, should have been expecting. A tap dance was performed for assuring users that what they thought they wanted was coming, later, and users should have understood that from the beginning. Left is right, up is down, at any cost users needed to be convinced all was well, even when things were seriously wrong. For IT, such reactions were simply a coping mechanism for survival. Sadly, those techniques do not hide things for very long. Those missteps and failures were why organizations ended up desperately searching for a new approach.

The inability to acknowledge failure can become a cultural norm within an organization. Such a force can derails Agile efforts. This *everything-is-success* perspective can pervert things. When users provide feedback about the latest deliverable not being what they want, an Agile team should accept that response, gather detailed information, and then use that newly acquired knowledge to correct the object under development. Agile techniques focus on delivering smaller pieces at a fast pace, so that failure of a single small unit is meant to be a small thing. The IT management needs to view these small deliverables as what they are. If instead, users are talked down to the solution really being what they want, or that the users do not appreciate how things must evolve, the only result is disengaged users. And disengaged users are exactly the opposite of what Agile approaches are trying to accomplish.

Accept failure. Failure happens far more frequently than most organizations are comfortable admitting. Although failure isn't the best thing, within Agile it can be the second best. Organizations wishing to go Agile need to back off from the usual flinch response of hiding failures. It is the fear of punishment that drives employing all the coverups, word parsing, and other evasive tactics. These shifty techniques are often the main cause behind business having bad thoughts about their IT partners. Look at each failure as an opportunity to improve both your IT deliverables and your understanding with the user community. These circumstances are indeed opportunities and should be embraced as such. Fail early to learn so you can better serve your customers.

After all, becoming proficient at any skill requires time, effort, and discipline, and the willingness to persevere through whatever difficulties may arise. Persistence is the key. Every time I make a mistake managing a project, I recognize and say, "I made a mistake. I will do all my best to correct my mistake. My apologies about that." It is the type of behavior I get across to my people. This attitude is very helpful in my life as a project manager. So, the greatest mistake of a project manager is not to recognize that something went wrong and not to say "I made a mistake."

The Power of Persistence

I believe commitment is the essence of a learning attitude. The key to getting what you want is the willingness to do "whatever it takes" to accomplish your objective. What do I mean by this willingness? It is a mental attitude that says: if it takes five steps to reach my goal, I'll take those five steps, but if it takes 30 steps to reach my goal, I will be persistent and take those 30 steps.

On most occasions in the project field, you don't know how many steps you must take to reach your goal or to accomplish your deliverables. This does not matter. To succeed, all that's necessary is that you make a commitment to do whatever it takes regardless of the number of steps or activities involved.

Persistent action follows commitment. You first must be committed to something before you'll persist to achieve it. Once you make a commitment to achieve your goal, then you will follow through with relentless determination and action until you attain the desired result. The most difficult thing I found is how to convince the team about the big impact on business that commitment within projects has on organizations. When you make a commitment and you are willing to do whatever it takes, including the effort to communicate a clear, convincing, and compelling message, you begin to attract the people and circumstances necessary to accomplish your goal.

I started my project management services company 16 years ago and have been persistent sending proposals and delivering presentations to my customers about our services. Every year I review my company strategy and insist again on the customers we are pursuing to do business with. My objectives are clear enough so I never give up. Sometimes I was successful and the customer recognized my persistence. Other times I did not achieve my goal but I tried to learn from that experience and insisted again and again, keeping a polite way with my customers all the time.

My Rules of Persistence

Therefore, today I have decided on some "rules of persistence for my projects and for myself" (Figure 4.3):

1. *No regrets*: I will follow my dreams to the fullest. With all my energy I will give it my complete will and effort. So that even if the desired result does not come about, I will have no regrets. I know I tried. I honor all decisions made that they came from my freedom to choose and that I accept the consequences.
2. *I will live and activate my dreams through little actions*: Yard by yard, push by little push. I need not take massive action each day. But a little measurable step forward will bring me that much nearer to my goal. For example, when I was writing this book, I tried to write a

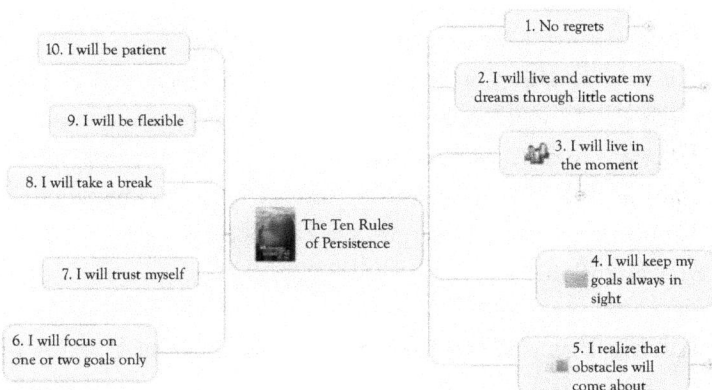

The Ten Rules of Persistence

10. I will be patient

9. I will be flexible

8. I will take a break

7. I will trust myself

6. I will focus on one or two goals only

1. No regrets

2. I will live and activate my dreams through little actions

3. I will live in the moment

4. I will keep my goals always in sight

5. I realize that obstacles will come about

Figure 4.3 The ten rules of persistence

little every day. I was not so productive on all days, but I moved forward a little bit.

3. *I will live in the moment*: Not in the past and not too much into the future. The full realization of the present will make the future come about on its own. Let me effuse all my energies on the present so that I don't rue the time lost when the clock ticks over. Work hard today and for sure you will build up a better tomorrow.

4. *I will keep my goals always in sight*: I have written down goals. I carry a copy with me in my wallet. I am making a daily habit of at least going through it once. The other places I have kept it is as a wallpaper on my monitor. It's always on my face and in my subconscious too.

5. *I realize that obstacles will come about*: I need to work around them. Goals are what lie behind all the stumbling blocks. If I cannot vault over them then I will walk around them. It might take longer but I will get around the block.

6. *I will focus on one or two goals only*: Focus is concentration on one single point. It's much easier to be persistent when we have clarity of a single goal. Too many goals dissipate our energies and loss of energy is always followed by loss of persistence.

7. *I will trust myself*: When others can do it, so can I. I try out this mantra every day. Every day for me is a good day, and I say that early in the morning every day. I know all the power to achieve my goals lies within me. I only have to harness it.

8. *I will take a break*: I have to fill myself up with energy. After every slight success it's important to taste a reward. Just to chill out for a while and then get back on the job rejuvenated.

9. *I will be flexible*: Constant action sometimes demands inconstant methods. If a way is not working too well, I will try to find out some other way to do it. There always is more than one way to skin the cat.

10. *I will be patient*: What defeats persistence is time. Time is our greatest friend as well as our greatest enemy. Persistent action by its very extension.

Acting Positive and with Passion Across Borders

My attitude is always positive, but some days my mood is not very good, then I need to do an attitude check (Bucero 2010). I wanted to share with you some of my best practices to be more positive in managing people in projects across organizations:

1. *Put a quote of the day on everyone's desk*: Thinking positive you can find quotes that can impact positively to your people. I usually say: "Clear expectations are the mother of motivation." You need to use positive and encouraging quotes every day. I have been using "the quote of the day" in most of the projects I managed, and after using it for some days I stopped sending it; immediately my team members came to me and asked, "Why did not you send the 'quote of the day' today?"

2. *Use positive language*: Every time I get a team assigned for a project, when establishing the norms for the team, I explain to them that using negative words is prohibited during the project. Based on that, we created our positive vocabulary. For instance, we used words and sentences like *I will learn how to do* and *How can we improve it?* Getting inspired by others and doing my best to find the time, we have to find resources. You can try it, and let's try another way.

3. *Be willing to do for others without measuring*: Be ready to serve others. You, as a project manager, need to help your project stakeholders. Use your generosity. Do not measure how many times you helped them. Just do it and you will receive your pay back.

4. *Be an example for others to follow*: Arrive first in the morning. Arrive first to your project meetings. Be proactive, never complain, and never give up when you have a clear objective to accomplish and if you believe it is possible, listen to your people and look for ways to learn from any project stakeholder. Be open and clear with your people and give the right feedback frequently. Ask them for feedback about you. You may believe you are a very good skilled communicator for example, but you need to ask for feedback to your audience and learn from it. Learn something every day.

5. *Ask one more question before you answer*: Breathe deeply and count from one to ten asking for clarification before answering a question from your people. They will pay attention on your reactions, so your words can make a difference. Please reflect on that.

6. *Do not join the pity party*: Do not join the complainers in your project or in your organization. There are some people who are only focused on complaining all the time but they never think about potential solutions. Look at the solutions or alternatives not at the problems. Think differently and be as positive as you can.

7. *Do not join the revolt*: When you find a hostile or unfair situation, be analytic and assess the situation before acting. Sometimes as leaders we are inclined to the action too soon. Be careful about that.

8. *Solve rather than complain*: Do not complain, take action, or try other way to solve your pains, issues, or problems. If you do not know how to solve the issue, ask for help from your team members, peers, and colleagues. Usually project managers are not wise men or women.

9. *Get the third party being talked about negativity into the conversation*: In many projects you will collaborate with third parties. Assess their attitude and ask them for an attitude check when needed.

You can be more positive than you are. Move forward and look at your future to improve your attitude. You need to act. Your positive attitude depends on you. Do not wait and start now because today is a good day but tomorrow will be better.

Using Your Creativity

Creativity is the art of contradiction (Dutton and Krausz 2014). It is an art, not science. In a different way, you are creating something different from what already exists. If you contradict what already exists, you enter into the creative world. Creativity is the act of turning new and imaginative ideas into reality. Creativity is characterized by the ability to perceive the world in new ways, to find hidden patterns, to make connections between seemingly unrelated phenomena, and to generate solutions. Creativity involves two processes: thinking and then producing.

What is the main reason for you to hire a leader in a company? The answer is to solve problems. Every organization has some problems, and every project manager has a few problems. If we did not have problems in organizations, the reason to hire project managers does not make sense.

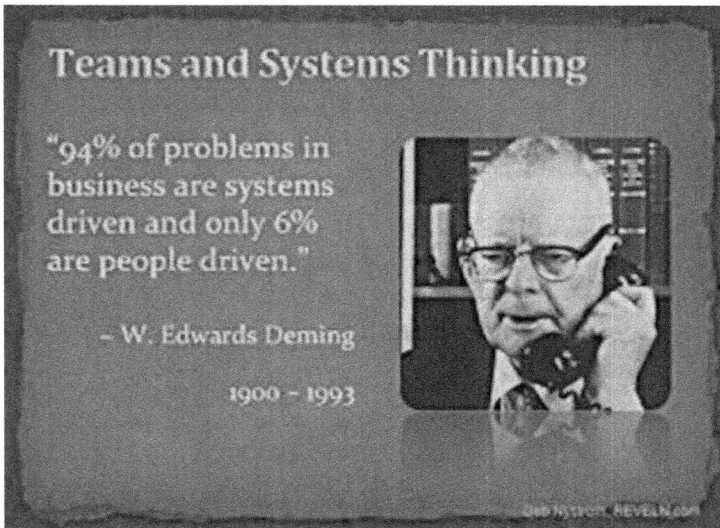

Figure 4.4 Think differently

But the 50 percent of the time of a leader needs to be focused on solving problems and the other 50 percent he or she needs to invent new problems to solve, by which I mean creating new ideas to be converted into projects.

The key is thinking differently (Figure 4.4). Look for a different way to do things in organizations. We need to learn to think and develop new ideas and approaches. Do not wait for creativity to come to you easily. Use your people, your team members, project stakeholders to create new things, new approaches, and new solutions.

Creativity is the process of bringing something new into being. Creativity requires passion and commitment. It brings to our awareness what was previously hidden and points to new life. Is this possible in business? I believe so, but you have to be willing to take risks and progress through discomfort to get to the finish line.

IBM's 2010 Global CEO Study stated:

"The effects of rising complexity call for CEOs and their teams to lead with bold creativity, connect with customers in imaginative ways and design their operations for speed and flexibility to position their organizations for 21st century success."

The Creativity Gap

A 2012 Adobe study on creativity (Lee et al. 2012) shows that eight in ten people feel that unlocking creativity is critical to economic growth and nearly two-thirds of the respondents feel creativity is valuable to society, yet a striking minority—only one in four people—believe they are living up to their own creative potential.

Can creativity be learned? The short answer is yes. A study by George Land reveals that we are naturally creative and as we grow up we learn to be uncreative. Creativity is a skill that can be developed and a process that can be managed.

Creativity begins with a foundation of knowledge, learning a discipline, and mastering a way of thinking. You can learn to be creative by experimenting, exploring, questioning assumptions, using imagination, and synthetizing information. Learning to be creative is akin to learning a sport. It requires practice to develop the right muscles and a supportive environment in which to flourish.

Studies by Clayton M. Christensen and his researchers uncovered the innovators' DNA: your ability to generate innovative ideas is not merely a function of the mind, but also a function of five key behaviors that optimize your brain for discovery:

1. *Associating*: drawing connections between questions, problems, or ideas from unrelated fields
2. *Questioning*: posing queries that challenge common wisdom
3. *Observing*: scrutinizing the behavior of customers, suppliers, and competitors to identify new ways of doing things
4. *Networking*: meeting people with different ideas and perspectives
5. *Experimenting*: constructing interactive experiences and provoking unorthodox responses to see what insights emerge

Richard Branson (English business magnate, investor, and philanthropist) has a mantra that runs through the DNA of Virgin companies. The mantra is A-B-C-D. (Always Be Connecting the Dots.) Creativity is a practice, and if you practice using these five discovery skills every day, you will develop your skills in creativity and innovation.

Happiness Assessment Tool

Project tension and stress provoke project managers that they don't smile too much when managing projects (Figure 4.5). As the global economy started a slow-down with many organizations announcing layoffs and closures, it is difficult for project managers and team members to remain positive and focused on their work. However, my experience is that smiling more and using good humor in projects can increase team member retention and workplace satisfaction.

On the other hand, some studies have shown that humor stimulates the right side of the brain, the side that supports thinking outside the box, which facilitates dealing with conflicts and problem-solving (Zey 2018). Good humor helps the project manager to be more creative and eliminate

Figure 4.5 Happiness

stress. Many colleagues asked me many times if I had a muscle problem in my face because I am always showing a smiling happy face.

Have you ever thought of measuring a smile? Most scientists invest in various studies regarding smiles, how much people mean it, and how different smiles can be distinguished. Advanced studies even have patterns to determine if your smile is fake or real.[1, 2] These studies based their results on facial muscles they identified to be responsible when a person is smiling. However, no matter how much studies were conducted, how many factors were considered, and how much results are shown, the question of measuring a smile is still a debatable topic.

So, can you really measure smile? How much joy does it give to your team members and other project stakeholders? In what angle or amount of mouth opening is to be considered as the best smile? How much pain can certain smiles eliminate? How long must someone smile in order to lessen negative feelings? All these questions together with some thousand questions about smiles are yet to be answered and remain a mystery to be unfolded. With the kind of technology that we have today, indeed experts can measure certain factors of smiles but no one can still decipher the smile itself.

After all, not everything in this world can be measured and that includes smile. Can you measure a smile?

Harvard psychology professor Daniel Gilbert is widely known for his 2006 best-seller, *Stumbling on Happiness*. His work reveals, among other things, the systematic mistakes we all make in imagining how happy (or miserable) we'll be.

Are you happy as a project manager?

How Is It Possible to Measure Something as Subjective as Happiness?

Measuring subjective experiences is a lot easier than you think. It's what your eye doctor does when he or she fits you for glasses. He or she puts a

---

[1] Harvard Business Review, Daniel Goleman, Annie McKee, Bill George, Herminia Ibarra.

[2] Scientific American. Spotting a Fake Smile. By Rachel Mahan, Clara Moskowitz, Siri Carpenter, Nicole Branan on February 1, 2009.

lens in front of your eye and asks you to report your experience, and then she puts another lens up, and then another. They use your reports as data, submits the data to scientific analysis, and designs a lens that will give you perfect vision—all on the basis of your reports of your subjective experience. People's real-time reports are very good approximations of their experiences, and they make it possible for us to see the world through their eyes. People may not be able to tell us how happy they were yesterday or how happy they will be tomorrow, but they *can* tell us how they're feeling at the moment we ask them. "How are you?" may be the world's most frequently asked question, and nobody's stumped by it.

There are many ways to measure happiness. We can ask people "How happy are you right now?" and have them rate it on a scale. We can use magnetic resonance imaging to measure cerebral blood flow, or electromyography to measure the activity of the "smile muscles" in the face. But in most circumstances those measures are highly correlated, and you'd have to be the federal government to prefer the complicated, expensive measures over the simple, inexpensive one.

What Did All These Happiness Researchers Discover?

Much of the research confirms things we've always suspected. For example, in general people who are in good romantic relationships are happier than those who aren't (Goleman et al. 2017). Healthy people are happier than sick people. People who participate in their churches are happier than those who don't. Rich people are happier than poor people. And so on.

That said, there have been some surprises. For example, while all these things do make people happier, it's astonishing how little any one of them matters. Yes, a new house or a new spouse will make you happier, but not much and not for long. As it turns out, people are not very good at predicting what will make them happy and how long that happiness will last. They expect positive events to make them much happier than those events actually do, and they expect negative events to make them unhappier than they actually do. In both field and lab studies, we've found that winning or losing an election, gaining or losing a romantic partner, getting or not getting a promotion, passing or failing an exam—all have less impact on happiness than people think they will.

A recent study showed that very few experiences affect us for more than three months (When good things happen, we celebrate for a while and then turn sober.) When bad things happen, we weep and whine for a while and then pick ourselves up and get on with it.

Will All This Research Ultimately Makes Us Happier?

We are learning and will continue to learn how to maximize our happiness. So yes, there is no doubt that the research has helped and will continue to help us increase our happiness. But that still leaves the big question: What kind of happiness *should* we want? For example, do we want the average happiness of our moments to be as large as possible, or do we want the sum of our happy moments to be as large as possible? Those are different things. Do we want lives free of pain and heartache, or is there value in those experiences? Science will soon be able to tell us how to live the lives we want, but it will never tell us what kinds of lives we should want to live. That will be for us to decide.

Researchers have attempted to measure happiness with five approaches:

1. *Biological* (Figure 4.6): If you come to my lab and I offer you a Popsicle, don't take it. Our freezer is filled with frozen specimens of undergraduates' saliva and urine. We're looking for the biological markers, such as hormones and neurotransmitters, for happiness. So far, researchers have had only minimal success in identifying the biological markers of happiness. What we do know is that the markers for happiness aren't the same as for depression. For example, if low levels of the neurotransmitter serotonin predict depression, high levels of serotonin don't predict happiness. This is important. It suggests that happiness and depression are not opposite ends of a single continuum, but are better thought of as related, but independent, dimensions.

2. *Behavioral*: Researchers have used behaviors to estimate happiness. Behaviors such as frequency of smiling, laughing, and helping others have been examined. When the use of emojis is studied, the results suggest that Hawaii is the happiest state, and Louisiana is the least happy. When hundreds of tweets are analyzed, researchers find that

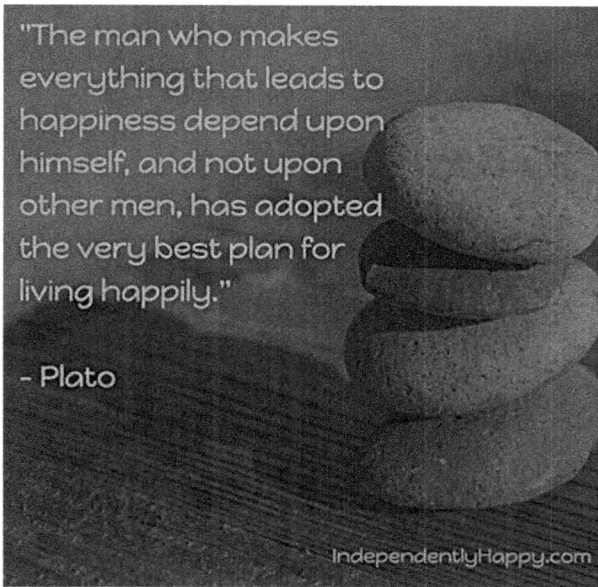

"The man who makes everything that leads to happiness depend upon himself, and not upon other men, has adopted the very best plan for living happily."

- Plato

IndependentlyHappy.com

Figure 4.6 Biological happiness

Mondays are linked to low levels of happiness, and daylight-saving time results in a happiness boost.

3. *Implicit measures*: Disguised measures, in which people don't even know that their happiness is being assessed, have been developed. These have been successfully used to assess racism. Implicit measures typically assess reaction times to connect positive and negative terms to oneself and to others. However, implicit measures haven't proved to be effective in assessing happiness.

4. *Other reports*: Asking others to rate a person's happiness has been useful. For example, for young children, we ask their parents and teachers to rate their children's happiness.

5. *Self-reports*: By far the most common way that researchers assess happiness is through self-reports. Using multiple-item scales or a single question, we simply ask people about their level of happiness. People think about their happiness and it is a subjective state, so it makes sense to ask them about their happiness. But this approach presents challenges. For example, when people were asked, "Looking back at your life as a whole, overall how happy are you?" The answers they

gave changed if they found a few coins at a photocopy machine that the researchers had planted there. Now, finding a few coins shouldn't have a significant impact on one's happiness when considering the past decades of one's life. But it does change the answers people give. We are disproportionately impacted by the most recent events of our lives.

The development of measures of happiness has allowed researchers to assess happiness. However, measuring happiness is not simple or easy.

Chapter Summary

The most interesting ideas to remember in this chapter are as follows:

- Be contagious as a positive mosquito in your project team, organization, and environment, and you will generate a more and more positive atmosphere.
- Considering that projects are uncertain endeavors, project teams and project managers achieve right or wrong results. Depending on the point of view of those teams and leaders, those results will be considered as failures or as opportunities to learn.
- The most important thing is how to move from failures to project success.
- The key to getting what you want is the willingness to do "whatever it takes" to accomplish your objective.
- My attitude is always positive, but somedays my mood is not very good, then I need to do an attitude check.
- Once you make a commitment to achieve your goal, then you will follow through with relentless determination and action until you attain the desired result.

References

Bucero, A. 2010. *Today is a Good Day: Attitudes for Achieving Project Success.* Multimedia Publications.

Dutton, D., and M. Krausz. 2014. *The Concept of Creativity in Science and Art.* Springer.

Gilbert, D. 2006. *Stumbling on Happiness.* New York, NY: A.A. Knopf.

Goleman, L., and M. Congleton. 2017. *Emotional Intelligence Collection.* Harvard Business Review.

Lee, J., N. Gu, J.R. Jupp, and S.M. Sherratt. 2012. *Towards a Formal Evaluation of Creativity in Parametric Design Process: A Pilot Study.* Design research Society.

McConnell, T. 2013. *The Nature of Disease: Pathology for the Health Professions.* Lippincott Williams & Wilkins.

Zey, M. 2018. *Seizing the Future: Dawn of the Macroindustrial Era.* Science.

CHAPTER 5

Learning Something Every Day

*Everybody could be my teacher. If you are an observer you will learn
something every day.*

—Alfonso Bucero

I believe learning is a need. One of the best ways to leverage your free
time in the upcoming year is to learn a new skill. Just think about the
most successful project professionals in the world. Those who consistently
succeed are those who are best at learning new skills.

I believe that successful people make the commitment to dedicate
their free time in the pursuit of learning. And they stick to their promise
of learning. With that in mind, there are countless things you can learn in
your free time. Prepare a list of valuable things to learn that will improve
your life—both personally and professionally. With this list it will not be
difficult to find those new skills to learn, but it will be difficult narrow-
ing down your list of what you want to learn. Learning is the process of
acquiring new skills. Please do not wait. Start today!

Today, the worlds of learning and personal or professional development are literally at your fingertips. The open learning movement has
made the opportunity to get smarter in your spare time completely acces-
sible to anyone with an Internet connection, and it has exploded in recent
years. Challenge yourself to learn something new every day. It can benefit
your career, your personal life, and your mental well-being, making you
a happier and more productive person overall. There are so many people
you can learn from as a project professional.

Of course, you may learn from different sources, as I will share with
you along this chapter.

Learn from Your Executives

I learned three lessons from my worst boss (Figure 5.1).

First, career leadership opportunities spark a special excitement. After several years of contemplating how you would do things differently and better, you finally have that chance to demonstrate your ability to make a difference.

There is danger in those thoughts, however. Too frequently, the emphasis shifts from a focus on the organization to a focus on your own vision of yourself as a leader. As the mirror turns inward, however, it fails to reflect everything else you need to see and understand in order to be the type of leader you once dreamed of becoming.

Despite the thousands of books and hundreds of thousands of articles written on the topic, I believe there are no secrets to being a successful leader. Every day, we witness the strengths and weaknesses of leaders in our workplaces, government, and communities. Their failures are generally obvious, yet their mistakes are repeated with remarkable consistency.

My advice to a first-time leader, therefore, is to be counterintuitive. Before reading all the books advising you on how to be a great leader, start by paying attention to the many bad leaders you have read about or observed. Understanding their failures will prove to be instructive. For starters, here are three key deficiencies you should avoid emulating.

Figure 5.1 Learn from your executives

1. *Speaking before thinking.* New leaders may want to quickly assert their authority and show their ability to act decisively. Avoid that impulse. You may have gotten this job, but the job is not about you. Some decisions may require speed and decisiveness but most benefit from collaboration and input.

2. *Avoiding negative feedback.* Most workplace managers dislike having to critique other people's performance. The default is to ignore the behavior and develop a workaround, rather than engage in an awkward conversation. Some even handle negative experiences by creating new rules that adversely affect everyone else in the workplace, hoping to change the offending employee through policy rather than direct discussion. This approach only succeeds in annoying good employees while leaving the source of the problem still clueless. Feedback is a skill that can be learned and used to the advantage of everyone in the workplace.

3. *Ignoring the benefits of diversity.* It is hard to believe that we have been having the same tired conversations about diversity for decades, while ignoring rapidly changing global demographics that will negatively impact those who do not change. The lack of progress in diversifying senior levels of leadership is the result of leaders who lack vision, commitment, and a willingness to implement some of the difficult and sophisticated steps needed to make a difference. It is no longer about the pipeline, nor is it about "fixing" the individuals who fall into the diverse categories. It is about putting in place the training and systems needed to understand and avoid the impacts of unconscious biases that negatively impact careers at every stage of employment. It is also about ensuring that the creation of an inclusive environment is a vital component of your organization's business strategy.

Then, as you assume that leadership mantle for the first time, pay attention to those bad leaders you have been watching for years. And then do the opposite. I also would like to share with you some lessons learned from my best manager (Figure 5.2).

My favorite manager in my professional career was a man named La Fuente, who managed the project presales at Digital Equipment

Figure 5.2 I love my boss

Corporation many years ago. Manager Mr. La Fuente was an employee favorite because he actually spent time on the project sales floor, helping all his employees rather than in his office analyzing stuff like unit per transaction figures. He was my favorite manager not only because we got along greatly, but because he actually seemed to value what I spoke. He always asked for my opinion on project sales solutions, which was something I quite enjoyed at the time.

Every week he spent 10 to 15 minutes with me to give feedback. He also asked me questions like, "What would you do different next time?" which always made me think about it a little harder. A lot of times my ideas were actually put into action, and every time that happened I would be filled with a sense of pride.

Mr. La Fuente really made me feel valued. I had a sense that he was honestly invested in me, and those feelings have stuck with me to this day, more than 30 years later. Some years later when I was working as a senior project manager, I found myself thinking what made Mr. La Fuente such a great manager.

What did I learn from him that I could now apply to my role as a project manager?

1. *Be available*—Managers need always to be available and not constantly locked away in an office or tied down by meetings. Most, if not all, of us have had a manager in the past who was not a part of

the team and hid away behind closed doors. Being an unavailable manager leads to poor morale and a lack of trust in the workplace. You do not want that. My next manager created a versus-him mentality. I did not trust my manager and I felt it was an unbalanced and unfair work environment. Manager La Fuente believed in his people. Whenever we were faced with a daunting task, he would roll up his sleeves, join us, and get to work. "It is the work environment and the feeling of being treated unfairly by the management that has the greatest effect on an employee's mood." Employees left with the burden of a huge workload without support will feel as if they're being treated unfairly by managers. Your team's morale is too valuable to not make time for them. Join the brainstorm session. Be part of the hack day. Just being available is a huge boost. A manager does not have to be clocked in 24/7, but having an open-door policy and being involved in the process should be expected. Making time for your team needs to be a top priority for any manager. Company culture, employee morale, and mood are all directly related to accessibility and availability of management.

2. *Listening*—The second thing I took away from Manager La Fuente was to listen. La Fuente had this way of making me feel like I was important, as if my thoughts and ideas were actually valuable to the entire company. Every time we spoke, I felt my ideas, feedback, or concerns were met with understanding and often followed by action. Listening is the first step in creating progress and overcoming obstacles. A good manager understands the roadblocks faced by his or her team and then works to overcome them.

Manager Mr. La Fuente had great listening skills. For some people it comes naturally; for others it takes some effort. A simple and actionable method for building those skills and the relationship with a team is to share what everyone is working on that day. Many managers already do this, but unknowingly fall short because they fail to share what they are working on with the rest of their team. This creates an uneven work environment and a sense of the employees not knowing what managers actually do. Every manager should be a great listener; it opens up channels of communication and can prevent an unhappy work environment.

3. *Understand your team's strengths*—The last lesson I took away from Mr. La Fuente is to understand your team's strengths and use those strengths to drive productivity. I believe each person has his or her unique set of skills and strengths. Manager La Fuente had the insight to see that I was actually interested in project management and he used that as a motivator. His insight not only increased my productivity, but also made me feel more valued at work.

A perfect example of this in action was that he offered me an opportunity to move to the project delivery department six months later, and I accepted and moved forward counting on his support. This insight can only be brought to light by a management team that is available to his or her employees and actively listens to not only what roadblocks are ahead, but also sees the strengths in each person.

Looking back, Manager La Fuente certainly left a big impression on me, and looking down the road, I want to be the type of manager who inspires people like he inspired me. Now it is your time to reflect upon. What manager left an impression on you? Share your stories of someone that left his or her mark on your career.

Leadership Lessons You Can Learn from Your Boss' Behavior

The working world's best and worst bosses have certain traits that define their leadership. From micromanaging compulsively to communicating poorly, a bad boss can drive you nuts and make you hate your job. On the other hand, a boss who knows how to properly motivate his/her staff leads a productive and satisfied team. The lessons you learn from these and other behaviors will eventually help you make the transition to project manager yourself.

Here are some good and bad behaviors to look out for in your boss. As you look for them, keep in mind what they could mean for your professional future as you look to grow into a leader.

Good: Sticks around at crunch time
When a deadline is looming, the best bosses recognize that their team will need to go fully heads down, take shorter lunch breaks, and work hard to get to the finish line. And when this happens, they do not go into hiding

or work at their normal pace. They stay along for the ride to help, provide guidance, and ultimately keep an eye on their employees' health and well-being. They even force them to go home and rest rather than burn themselves out. They work as hard as anyone else, but when it comes time to rest, they're the first to tell everyone to go home and refresh.

If your boss sticks around, works hard, and provides moral support during a deadline, you end up learning two important things for your career. First, you learn that the manager's responsibility to their team is to set a smart and healthy example so that everyone's at their best. And second, you learn that a healthy and stress-free team performs better. This understanding will help you become a great people manager yourself when you make that career leap. In the short run, it will also discourage you from harming yourself by constantly burning the midnight oil.

Bad: Does not take the heat from higher-ups
Ever go to a meeting with your boss and your boss's boss having to explain why a project fell apart? In these cases, it is often one individual who gets singled out and is given grief. This type of situation can seed resentment and stress, especially when the problem is a result of systemic failure across an entire team rather than the mistake of a single person.

The best bosses understand that part of their job is to take the heat when things go wrong. They act as a shield around their staff, assigning punishment and giving hard talks themselves. Meanwhile, they show explicitly to the people they report to that the buck stops with them. If your boss is more than happy to expose you and your colleagues to anger from higher management, they are showing that they'd rather save their own skin than lead and teach by example. In the end, this results in frustration and anger at work, which can lead to high turnover and a lack of job satisfaction.

Good: Lets others lead
Does your boss always open and lead every meeting or do they pick someone else to run it in their stead? Do they insist on closing every sale or being in on every conversation or do they give you and your colleagues autonomy? If your answer to either of these is the latter, you have a good boss who understands that they cannot simply take point on everything.

They instead help their employees to develop into confident workers and leaders by providing leadership opportunities.

A boss who gives you and your team leadership opportunities regularly recognizes that they are in part responsible for your career progression. They have learned from their mentors and bosses in the past about how to let others take charge. Now they are passing that knowledge down to you. As a result, you are gaining crucial leadership experience that will enable you become a manager yourself. You're also learning how to build and manage a team of employees that consider you a mentor.

Bad: Promotes divisive competition

Some of the worst bosses in the world lead by dividing rather than enabling collaboration. Whether by driving cutthroat competition between colleagues or by pitting an entire team against one individual, the end result is a lack of trust and severe inefficiency.

Find yourself constantly angry at another teammate? Struggling to compete and cut corners rather than get things done the right way? This kind of behavior can get really frustrating really quickly and, is likely enforced from the top down. Your boss is creating a culture that values a divided team over a solid unit.

For your own development as a leader, understand that healthy competition should be fun and collaborative. You do not need to ignore competition altogether, but it should be done as a way to lift the output of the team as a whole rather than reward one or two top performers. A good way to do this is to have top performers help and train those who are lagging behind. That way, everyone learns and no one is left behind.

Good: Keeps everyone in the loop

A great boss understands that their team can only work as efficiently as possible if they understand the implications, potential outcomes, and motivations behind a project. They know that sharing the strategy and logic behind the work they assign results in better output and fewer mistakes. They also understand that a project cannot fully succeed if competing ideas are not brought to light. That's why they ask for opinions and implement ideas from their staff.

This is a great behavior to model your own future leadership skills after. It focuses on the idea that a team is full of equals who don't just deserve to know the intricacies of their work. They also work better when they have a good idea of what everyone else around them is doing. Less miscommunication occurs and less time is wasted fixing directionless work. As a result, the team succeeds with collaborative effort rather than failing with misfitting individual contributions.

Bad: Delegates inefficiently
Some bosses fail to delegate whatsoever and end up either piling a ton of work on one person or just trying to do everything themselves. Others, more dangerously, delegate inefficiently by failing to recognize the strengths and weaknesses of their team. Does your boss often give tasks that sound perfect for your skillset to a colleague who needs to be trained to do them? Do you regularly get tasks that sound way outside the reasonable bounds of your job description?

If you are doing tasks that are not fit for your skillset, you understand how frustrating and demotivating work can get. What you can learn from this type of boss is that how closely you evaluate the talent around you dictates how well they'll do the tasks you give them. If you take care to understand how and why your teammates' talents are misused by your current boss, it will help you delegate in a way that will keep your future employees happy and productive.

Your best example for how to lead (and how not to lead) is the person who manages you today. Look at what they do and how they behave. Understand how those attitudes affect their employees. Use the lessons you learn from this evaluation to become a great leader yourself.

Learn from Your Peers and Colleagues

Ever since I joined the world of project management, I have had the good fortune of learning from more experienced team members and project managers. Their mentorship has given me the opportunity to learn and grow as a project manager over the years. I am grateful for the help and support from those colleagues and managers. Documenting all of the takeaways from the mentors I have had would be impossible, but these are a few of the most significant ones.

1. *Fight for your project*:
   Many projects do not go smoothly. Change is hard, and countless factors can get in the way. Do not let them stop you. As the project manager, it is your role to fight for the viability of your project. Your project goals, timelines, and teams must be carefully monitored and defended. Although you likely will not get your way all the time, you will win the trust of clients and project teams by not passively accepting threats to your project.

2. *Communication is key*:
   Do not assume nothing. They are essential (after all, you need to start somewhere), but it is also essential that you discuss, document, and keep your assumptions in check. Communication uncovers assumptions that you and your project team may not know you had. Lack of communication can leave them buried and can lead to nasty surprises down the road.

3. *Stay ahead of the curve*:
   It is easy to get wrapped up in a project's day-to-day aspects. There are so many timelines, resources, people, and expectations flying around that they can become all-consuming. Do not let them be. Always keep the objectives and end-goal of your project in mind. Keep an eye out for the lessons learned that will strengthen your next project.

4. *Know what you don't know*:
   The best project managers I know are continuous learners. They have taught me to develop enough expertise to be effective and conversational in a variety of related fields. But they also emphasized that each of us needs to know our limits and recognize when you need to involve a subject matter expert.

5. *Change is the only constant*:
   As project managers, we plan and then work with stakeholders to implement our plan. But we must always stay mindful of enterprise environmental factors. The world around us is changing at a dizzying pace. New technologies roll out that may make your projects more

or less challenging. New methods of communication may impact how your project team works together (hopefully for the better). If you are not changing with the world around you, your skills and your project may quickly become obsolete.

6. *Get to know your team*:

    Project management can certainly be stressful. But it is fun! You have the unique opportunity to interact with people and groups inside and outside your department and organizations. Take the time to get to know them and what makes them tick! Beyond what you learn from them, good relationships can help you through challenging times. What have you learned from your mentors along the way? And in turn, what lessons would you most like to pass along to your current or future mentees?

Learn from Your Wife or Partner

I had not had serious relationships before meeting my girlfriend, now my wife. I thought I was an adult; I thought I knew how to be a great boyfriend. Meeting someone I had a serious connection with taught me that nothing I had experienced before was real. True love feels different than casual relationships, even if those relationships lasted for years. When you are in a good relationship, you learn things. You act differently; you think as part of a team, not as an individual making your way through the world. You will be more understanding and accepting of your partner, instead of just getting frustrated with them like you may have with past relationships.

1. *Misunderstandings are inevitable*:

    Misunderstandings are going to happen. If you take your partner's words one way, then learn they meant something totally different, don't punish them (Bucero 2015). Let it go. Bringing it up all the time is only going to bruise the relationship and cause communication problems later. Sometimes what you say or do will be taken the wrong way, and you'll get frustrated that your partner doesn't understand. Take a step back and realize it's not a big deal. Misunderstandings are made to be swept under the rug because they're so minor. They only become problems if you let them grow bigger and mean more in the scope of your relationship. Be laid back and forgive misunderstandings.

2. *Learn to trust them*:

You have to trust your partner. Why would you share your life with someone when you think they're doing something wrong every time you turn your back? If you don't trust your partner to be faithful, honest, caring, or anything else, then you're not in a good relationship. The best relationships begin with a deep trust, and even if problems come up (and they will!), the trust is strong enough to keep you together.

3. *Let yourselves miss each other*:

You're in love, so you want to be together all the time! It's so fun to cuddle all night and be together all day, but when will you have time to experience different things? When you go to separate workplaces or schools, you experience things that will give you something to talk about later. When you go out with your friends and your partner spends time with theirs, you have time and space to yourself and come back to each other refreshed. You have a chance to miss each other, and it helps you really understand the value of your relationship. Missing someone is great because getting to see them after that period will make you so happy and so sure of your relationship.

4. *Encourage growth and change*:

In a good relationship, both partners are encouraged to grow and change. You have one life to live—you need to explore it to the fullest! If you want to quit your job and go back to school, your partner should support you. If you want to try something new or go back to something old, you should find support in your relationship. And you should give this support in return. Encourage your partner to explore hobbies and interests and meet new people. If you want your partner to stay the same, you are going to have a very boring life together.

5. *Compromising does not mean you are weak*:

Compromising does not mean "giving in." It does not mean that you have lost the fight. In fact, it is the opposite. Do you know how hard it is to compromise sometimes? You want your way because it sounds right and makes sense to you. Your partner is way off base with their suggestions. Take a step back and look at the argument diplomatically. What's the logical conclusion? If your partner is right, don't be afraid to say so. Accept their way or modify both of your solutions to be half and half. The important thing is not getting your way, it is staying in your relationship and helping it grow. Compromising will definitely help your relationship grow.

6. *Admit your weaknesses*:

   Your partner does not expect you to be a superhero, and hopefully you do not expect that of them! We are all human; we all have flaws. It is ok to let these show. In fact, to have a stable, serious relationship, you need to let your weaknesses be known. Your partner will be more sensitive to things that bother you and can help build you up in areas where you need some help.

7. *Sometimes you can only accept things, not fix them*:

   People have baggage. You have some. Your partner has some. Can you go back and erase all of this? Nope! You're stuck with it and have to learn to deal with it. Some things are easier to get over than others, but the reality is that sometimes you can't fix things. You can't make problems go away. You have to accept them and get over them and move on, or else your relationship will crumble.

8. *Forgive quickly and truly*:

   Whenever you have a fight, don't worry about who wins or who loses. Learn from the fight—from what was said as much as from how it was resolved. Once you learn from a fight, you can apply that lesson to your relationship to avoid trouble later. That's all well and good, but you're not done! Forgive your partner! Forgive yourself. The fight is over and you're past it; now let it go. Never hold anything against your partner because the resentment will build until you don't want to be with them.

9. *Never expect anything*:

   Do not expect your partner to read your mind or to bring you breakfast in bed, or to offer to wash the dishes. It's not going to happen. You cannot expect anything from anyone—you have to make it known. Communicate. Make sure your partner knows what you expect from the relationship, as well as your opinions on a wide variety of issues. This will help them act considerate toward you, but still do not expect anything!

10. *Show your feelings*:

The worst thing you can do in a relationship is play games. Do not tease your partner; do not "reward" good deeds with love and affection. You have to make sure your partner always feels loved. You can be happy with them or be mad at them; it does not matter. They just need to feel loved. They need to know your feelings in the moment as well; don't get me wrong. But make sure you're showing your feelings in a way that they won't be misunderstood (back to #1!).

Learn from Your Stakeholders

My attitude is always positive. But somedays my mood is not very good, then I need to do an attitude check. The project management industry has put a lot of focus in recent years on the importance of stakeholder relationships. Project management practitioners and leading thinkers in the field have emphasized that a good project manager isn't just someone who is good at keeping track of all the tasks that need to be completed. A good project manager is also someone who can balance stakeholder needs and interests and ensure that all parties pull together and support the project in delivering a valuable outcome.

But how does the project manager make this happen?

1. **Understand who the stakeholders are.**

The first step in building great relationships with project stakeholders is to understand who they are. Many projects get delayed or end up not delivering the value they promised because the project manager failed to identify and engage all of the stakeholders. This means that essential requirements, needs, or insights might have been missed.

To find out who all the stakeholders could be, brainstorm groups and individuals who have an interest in the project or who will be affected by it. Whenever you identify a stakeholder, ask them if there's anyone else they believe you need to speak to. Keep going until you're sure you have identified all of them.

2. **Pinpoint stakeholders with high levels of power and influence.**

If you are leading a large project, you won't be able to spend an equal amount of time with every stakeholder. Naturally, you will have to engage and learn about every group or person you have identified, but the people you need to concentrate your efforts on those with the most power and influence.

Look at all the stakeholders on your list and assess who the three to five most impactful people are, that is, those who have the power to define your project, who can affect its direction, and who can help move it forward. Always make sure that your relationships with these influential decision makers are the best that they can be.

3. **Engage in one-to-one conversation.**

Building great relationships isn't about the amount of time you spend with someone, but about the quality of that time. Consider for instance how many people you interact with in meetings without knowing much about them. Great relationships are built through one-to-one conversations where you can find out more about what makes each person tick. Stakeholders are busy people, so respect their time by keeping your discussions as short as possible. Come prepared and let them know that the purpose of the meeting is to uncover anything that can help the project be successful—including how the two of you will be working together.

4. **Seek to understand their world.**

At the most fundamental level, project stakeholders will only open up to you and trust you when they feel that you understand them and that you have their best interests at heart. Your most important task is to enquire about their stake in the project, their requirements, and any knowledge or experience they have that can help deliver an outcome that adds more value.

Ask stakeholders what a successful project looks like in their eyes, such as:

- What their hopes and concerns are;
- How they would like you to keep them updated throughout the project;
- If a weekly status report will suffice; or
- They'd prefer a regular phone call.

Be curious and find out as much as you can about each person and their communication preferences.

5. **Communicate with clarity and honesty.**

To deepen the level of trust between you and each stakeholder, it's imperative that you communicate with clarity and honesty and that you don't sweep anything under the rug. Your stakeholders want to know what the *true* state of the project is, how it affects them, and if there is anything they can do to help.

Send out weekly or bimonthly status reports with an executive summary, an overview of which milestones have been delivered and which ones are still outstanding. Include the project's top five risks and issues with actions and owners. Similarly, conduct a monthly steering committee presentation where you talk about the real status of the project and what support you need from the committee members, if any, to overcome roadblocks and move the project forward.

6. **Continuously demonstrate your competence.**

Building good relationships with project stakeholders is not a one-off exercise or something that only happens at the beginning of the project. Continuously walking your talk and delivering on your promises will help you to further develop each relationship.

This can be done by demonstrating that you are a reliable and competent project manager—someone who is skilled at defining the project, locking down scope, creating a realistic plan, capturing requirements, managing risks, tracking the budget, and understanding the context of the business you are operating in. You can also demonstrate your competence by keeping meetings on track, capturing agreements and decisions, and holding people accountable for their actions.

Excellent stakeholder relationships can be built through one-to-one conversations where you take an interest in each person's world and help them get their needs fulfilled through the project. Be as open and honest as you can in your communication and treat your stakeholders like a valued client who you would like to be of service to.

Look at Your Mirror Every Day

One of my best practices is looking at my mirror every day and being aware of what you see and feel. What I mean is that we need to start the day with a positive attitude (see Figure 5.3). Nobody is able to see his/her neck. Every day if you are an observer, you will learn something that you can improve from your behavior in front of your peers, colleagues or project stakeholders.

However, some day we are tired or exhausted and our mind creates obstacles to stay as positive as we could. What to do?

My suggestion is to start the day charging your batteries. There are several methods to do it. Mine is as follows:

- I say thank you because a new day has started, I'm alive, my family is fine or any other positive reasons I can find.
- I repeat "Today is a good day."
- I do some physical exercise.
- I laugh a little bit under the shower.

Figure 5.3 Look into the mirror

My recipe does not need to be yours. You need to create your own recipe to move forward. That way works well for me every day. Even when you believe a particular day was not a good day for you, please look at the full part of the bottle and I am sure you will find something that will help you to move forward with a smile. Every obstacle you find is always a great opportunity to discover the wonderful things that life offers us.

Learning Assessment Tool

Most of us assume it's up to someone else to measure how much we have learned. But when we do this, we lose something very valuable: our own educational narrative. We may remember which subjects we excelled in and which subjects we failed or recall when and where we learned particular bits of information, but for the most part we cannot make sense of our learning as one long, unfolding event. And cognitive science has confirmed that the whole is, quite crucially, more than the sum of its parts.

Many employers complain that today's graduates seem to have learned nothing at university. But we know it's not for lack of trying, because many students have the same complaint. So how can this be? How is it that so many students spend four years "learning," only to graduate with scattered knowledge about a handful of topics?

One problem is the limited nature of human memory, and the fact that our assessment systems don't compliment the way the brain works. For example, teachers should be testing students more frequently to support retention, and with different media to help forge more connections. They should be discouraging the use of highlighters and the practice of rereading and encouraging self-quizzing and spaced study sessions.

Another issue seldom visited but equally important is that students aren't encouraged to assess their own learning. Instead, they're taught to memorize a unit here and a unit there, each one discrete and self-contained, then wait for a grade from some higher authority. That grade is meant to reflect how much a learner knows about a subject, and as soon as it's administered, however accurately, it stands as a permanent label of progress, not to mention potential. Shouldn't each of us, with our unique backgrounds and study habits, have the most authority on our progress? Shouldn't it be easiest for us, as individual learners, to determine our strengths and weaknesses in order to improve? When we assess our own progress, learning becomes one fluid process, whereby courses connect and build off each other, even years apart.

We can see where we've been and where we're going, and why it may take longer to achieve one goal versus another. It's not that we should have the only word on our progress—outside feedback is necessary and good—but we do need to be part of the conversation. And when we are, it's not only our motivation that receives a boost, but also our brain.

Why Self-Assessment Is Good for the Brain?

Imagine for a moment that, upon entering the public education system, everyone is required to create a personal learning portfolio, meant to last through university. In the portfolio are the usual samples of work, graded assignments, and notes. But there are also journal entries, hundreds of them, documenting your thoughts and reflections on what you have (and haven't) learned. Imagine being able to go back and read these entries, one year or 10 years later, to reflect on your learning journey as a whole. How might this influence the way you approach learning in general?

Researchers divided employees in a job training program into groups, and for ten days of the program, some of the employees were asked to reflect on what they had learned for 15 minutes each day. When the employees were given assessments at the end of their training, those in the reflection groups performed 23 percent better than those who hadn't been given time to reflect, according to reports. According to the researchers, reflection leads to a stronger feeling of self-efficacy, which in turn leads to improved performance.

"When we stop, reflect, and think about learning, we feel a greater sense of self-efficacy," Francesca Gino, one of the study's authors, told *Forbes*. "We're more motivated and we perform better afterward."

Author Preston says, "We think replaying memories during rest makes those earlier memories stronger, not just impacting the original content, but impacting the memories to come." "Nothing happens in isolation," says Preston. "When you are learning something new, you bring to mind all of the things you know that are related to that new information. In doing so, you embed the new information into your existing knowledge."

So, there you have it. Reflection is not some wishy-washy, new-age teaching strategy meant to bore students to death. It actually improves performance. And that's why it's such a powerful tool in the learning process. Reflection helps us organize, make sense of, and better remember what we've learned. Following are five ways self-assessment through reflection can aid learning.

Benefits of Self-Assessment

I want to summarize some of the benefits from self-assessment:

1. Interpreting

   Interpretation is a fundamental part of learning, but rarely do we take the time to interpret the learning process itself. Did it take you very long to learn a new concept? Would more context or background have helped? Are you finished studying or do you need another session? Interpreting your own learning helps you recognize patterns and habits that you can adjust for optimal retention.

2. Organizing:

   Most of us do not take the time to mentally organize individual concepts into more general patterns of cause-and-effect, or to break large concepts down into smaller points. Usually it's an instructor's job to do this as he or she designs a lesson, but there's no guarantee it will be done effectively. The advantage of self-assessment is that you can give yourself the opportunity to organize information however you want. The result is stronger connections between concepts and, ultimately, better learning.

3. Connecting:

   When you assess your own learning, you make connections between all sorts of things you wouldn't otherwise think about. You see the relationships between learning environment, study habits, instructional methods, subject matter, and so on., and over time it becomes possible to manipulate these factors in order to best suit your learning preferences.

4. Guiding:

   Once you reflect on what you've learned, what you haven't, and what you'd like to, you will have a much better idea of how to guide your own learning. And you'll save yourself a ton of time. Imagine sitting down to study for the Graduate Record Examination (GRE) and having a written summary of your strengths and weaknesses in algebra, which you recorded four years ago while studying for the Student Aptitude Test (SAT). What a time-saver!

5. Retaining:

How often do we "repeat history" when it comes to learning? And how often is it because we haven't reviewed or used a piece of information since we first learned it? The more we think about something we've learned—whether through written, spoken, or reflective means—the more likely we are to remember it.

The 10 Essentials of Self-Assessment

At the most fundamental level, self-assessment is about being more aware. You could call it mindfulness or metacognition, self-reflection or introspection, whatever term makes the most sense to you. The important thing is that you take the time to do it, and once you've gotten yourself into the habit of it, it will be easier to view learning as something you have control over.

Here are the ten steps I suggest you begin with:

1. Record what you know and what you don't:

You can determine the right time to do this for yourself, whether it's after a study session, a lecture, or even a test. The point is to do it, because most of us don't. Most of us passively absorb information in the hopes of retaining it, and this is simply not enough.

2. Measure notes taken against material remembered:

Is there a positive correlation between the amount of notes you take, and the amount of information you remember come test time? If not, you may want to rethink your note-taking habits, especially since you are sacrificing your attention to the lecture if you are constantly writing things down. Maybe you should try tape-recording the lecture instead and writing notes later.

3. Test yourself frequently and in different ways:

You won't really know what you know until you test yourself. So, do it frequently, daily even, and in different formats. If you used flashcards yesterday, challenge yourself to give a mini-lecture on it today. The more variety, the better your brain will remember it.

4. Measure retention over time:

   If the goal is to retain information for as long as possible, you'll need to keep reviewing it occasionally over time. This is where learning portfolios can really help. But you'll need to start seeing beyond midterms and finals, toward real-world situations in which you can use the material to your advantage. (If you can recall it in 10 years' time, that is…)

5. Note your interest level:

   The courses you struggle with are not always the courses you find uninteresting. And the courses you find uninteresting aren't always the ones you struggle with. When you don't get the grades you want, identify what the real reason is and take steps to solve the problem yourself.

6. Test your ability to relay information to others:

   This is the "true test" in my opinion. If you can't explain a concept to someone else, you haven't really learned it.

7. Connect new material with prior knowledge:

   This is something only you can do, despite how much background or context an instructor tries to provide. You are the only one who knows your "proximal zone of development," and therefore the only one who can connect new material with prior knowledge in a way that helps you remember both.

8. Test recall out of context:

   Why is it so hard to answer trivia questions? Because they force you to produce information out of context. But that's exactly what makes a champion quiz player so impressive: the ability to recall a detail or fact completely out of the blue, without associative clues or the original context in which it was first learned. One memory technique, called interleaved practice, suggests that alternating flashcards from different subjects within the same study session is actually better than keeping the subjects separate.

9. Make progress more personal:

   "Progress" is not about test scores and grades; it's about learning. Becoming more involved in our own learning early on, through a personal portfolio or other means, will make it easier to actually care about it and to think of it as an ongoing, interconnected process.

10. Measure study habits against results:

There's no use employing the same study strategy time after time if it doesn't work. So how do you know whether it works or not? Your test results and grades should give you some indication. But while most of us simply aim to "study harder" next time, we should instead aim to "study differently," acknowledging that progress is in our control.

Chapter Summary

From the ideas and concepts that were shown in this chapter, I would like to remark some of them:

- Those who consistently succeed are those who are best at learning new skills.
- Today, the worlds of learning and personal or professional development are literally at your fingertips.
- After several years of contemplating how you would do things differently and better, you finally have that chance to demonstrate your ability to make a difference.
- Fight for your project, communication is key, stay ahead of the curve, know what you know, and what you do not know.
- Change is the only constant.
- Get to know your team.

Reference

Bucero, A. 2015. *The Influential Project Manager: Winning Over Team Members and Stakeholders*. Boca Raton, FL: CRC Press.

CHAPTER 6

Growing Up Your Relationships

The meeting of two personalities is like the contact of two chemical substances: if there is any reaction, both are transformed.

—Carl Jung

You are not alone. As a project manager you need to work through people, so you need to grow up your relationships step by step. Establishing and creating relationships is like planting seeds in a garden. But what is necessary for your plants to grow up? You need to feed up them, add water, fertilize, and place where they receive some sunlight. Then it happens the same with your relationships; the point is not only to establish them, you need to maintain and sustain them through periodical contact.

You need insight into what is the chemical substance that helps you to get a positive reaction among people. You can attract people; your charismatic skills are there but you need to wake up them, perhaps to improve them. In the book *The Complete Project Manager* (Englund and Bucero 2014), some best practices are suggested about improving your charisma, and your personal and professional influence skills. For instance, if you want to influence somebody help him or her to achieve one of their objectives. That way your relationships will grow up more and more. In this chapter, I will be sharing with you some aspects to be considered to increase and get your relationships growing up; but you are responsible to get it done, and it is up to you to dedicate time and effort to follow through the steps I am proposing you.

Take Care of Your Contacts

Ever notice how moving forward in your career comes down to networking? The importance of career networking shouldn't be discounted when you are in the midst of a job search. In fact, career networking should become a part of your daily work and career-related endeavors.[1] Your career network should be in place for when you need it, both for job searching and for moving along the career ladder. Since you never know when you might need it, it makes sense to have an active career network, even if you don't need it today. That makes all those business cards you have collected and "LinkedIn connections" you have made extremely important. If you are not present in social media on the 21st century, as a business person or as a practitioner, you do not exist. The tricky part, however, is keeping in touch with your network of former colleagues and clients in a genuine way, so you don't come off as self-serving or stalker-like.

Part of it means maintaining some level of regular contact, so you're never in a position where it's been years since you've connected, and suddenly, in the middle of a job hunt, you have to send a sheepish "remember me?" e-mail. The rest is all about reaching out in an appropriate way depending on your relationship with your contact, so you strengthen your connections and can tap them for help when you need it. Let these tips show you how to walk the line between authentic and opportunistic.

I proposed some best practices:

1. *Reach out on social media*:
   Finally, a legit reason to spend time on Facebook, LinkedIn or Instagram during the workday: These and other social media sites allow you to get your name in front of old and new connections in an unobtrusive way. As you scroll through your feed, keep an eye out for profile updates or posts from your connections that announce a promotion, new company direction, or a career milestone. Craft a very short post congratulating them on their achievement, along the lines of "so excited for you" or "way to go!" At a loss for words? just hit the "like" button.

   Cheering on your contacts on social media lets them know you stand behind them.[2] Yet you're not asking them for anything in

---

[1] Doley, A. 2018. Learn About the Importance of Career Networking. Career Advice. Career networking.

[2] Clark, D. Marketing strategy consultant and author of Stand Out Networking: A Simple and Authentic Way to Meet People on Your Own Terms.

return and there's no expectation of a reply. They see your name, and that puts you on their radar. You'll also be noticed by their own contacts and that recognition can pay off down the road.

2. *Schedule regular check-ins*

For closer contacts, like a former mentor or key client you have worked with many times, I suggest you don't wait for them to post something online; some people just don't participate in social media that way. Instead, take the initiative by sending them a regular e-mail or message, say, every 60 days or once per quarter. The note doesn't have to be anything more than, "How's it going?" or an "I saw this article and thought of you" message with a link to an industry publication. The goal is to check in and get your name on their screen in a friendly, casual way.

And though it sounds a little impersonal, make it even easier to check in by using an app like "Contactually or Refer.com." Both track your contacts and prompt you to reach out based on time intervals you set. Refer.com even drafts the actual text of the message for you, based on the relationship level you have with that person, so you don't waste time searching for the right words.

3. *Plan small get-together*

Arranging for a face-to-face catchup with each contact individually is an impractical time suck. The solution: Set up small gatherings for a handful of people who all know each other. This way your crew of former coworkers from a past workplace, for example, can get together for a lunch or happy-hour outing. The group get-together works for a few reasons. First, it saves everyone time and energy. Second, you avoid the discomfort that sometimes happens when you are sitting across the table with one contact you have not seen in a while and no longer have much to talk about. A good practice is to take a new initiative or project inviting some volunteers to participate. I usually do that activity in my PMI local chapter. That way I have the opportunity to meet members from your professional association that you never met before.

4. *Show your gratitude*

Arranging for a face-to-face catchup with each contact individually is an impractical time suck. If one of your contacts taught you a valuable career lesson or helped you resolve a tricky issue, show your appreciation by sending them a note. Handwritten note always comes off as more personal and meaningful. But in today's digitally connected world, an e-mail or social media post can be appropriate as well.

Do not worry if they did their good deed a while ago; there's no expiration date when it comes to praise. I think people appreciate follow-up and kudos whenever they come, even if it's months after the fact. You could write something like, "Thanks so much to @ englund for the great advice on blogging a few months ago."

If someone went above and beyond, say they helped you land a new job or client, consider sending an actual gift such as a book on their favorite subject or just a note or letter of appreciation. It's a way to acknowledge them and say thank you. (Bucero 2010).

5. *Share your talent*

Offering to do a business-related favor—for example, arrange an e-mail introduction with an industry leader you know, or posting a Facebook link to a contact's latest podcast—conveys generosity. Most people tend to wait to network until they need something rather than reaching out authentically and genuinely. Instead, take the initiative and offer to help.

Get the ball rolling by asking, "Tell me, who is your ideal client? I may know some people you should meet,". Or, "What kind of investors are you looking to get on board? I'd like more clarity in case I come across an opportunity for you." Offering an assist will give you a rep as someone who is positive and wants others to thrive.

6. *Always update your contact list*

Just do not wrap up something with your company logo on it. "That is not a gift—it is a promotional item." People get promoted, marry, move away, and switch specialties all the time. Keep up with all the shifts by creating a Google doc or spreadsheet that lists all your contacts by name and includes what they do and how you met—and update it every time something changes. By the same token, make sure any page or site that lists your professional details—your job title, company name, and contact information—also reflects your current responsibilities, so people can easily reach you and get an accurate sense of what you have done in your career and currently do.

7. *Give them space*

    Staying close to business contacts means knowing when to back off. "If a colleague is really overwhelmed, it's a nice gesture to periodically send them an e-mail or leave a voice message and add, 'No need to respond.'" This shows a lot of respect for their schedule, because they may be too busy to get back to you and likely feel guilty about it. It frees them up and lets them know you simply want to check in and show that you care.

But what if you have reached out several times and continue to hear crickets? Only follow-up again if you have a good reason. People are busy, so it would be foolish to write someone off if you did not hear back from them once or twice, they could be traveling or having personal issues that make it difficult to respond.

At the same time, you have to accept that you might have been dumped from their network. If they ignore three messages sent over a span of time, especially if you have particular questions in your notes, then you can assume they do not want to keep up with you. Do not sweat it—just move on.

Try to Be Invited to Other Business Unit Meetings

As a project manager you need to establish, maintain, and sustain relationships with your colleagues, peers, and other project stakeholders. One of my best practices is trying to be invited to other business meetings (Englund and Bucero 2012). That way you may learn about other business pains and issues. You as a project manager need to know about it because perhaps some people from other businesses will be assigned to the project you need to manage.

    Let me give you an example. I looked to be invited to sales meetings in order to explain the sales people how to sell better solutions to customers (Figure 6.1). I proposed my initiatives and ideas to sales people but I also listened to their worries and sales targets. Mutual understanding was key to move forward and selling more and more successful projects; that way they were selling more and more and it was their sales department objective. Other example was getting invited to the support department

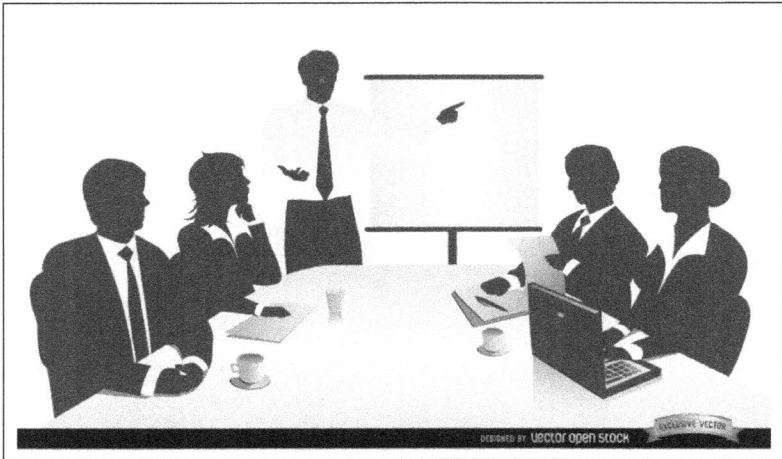

Figure 6.1 Business unit meetings

meetings. I worked for the project and consulting services department. We designed customer solutions projects but obviously those solutions needed to be supported by the support people. To be involved more and more with support department was really great because every designed solution from my department, before being sold, was tested to be feasible in order to be well supported. What was the result? To sell more solutions and support contracts.

For many years of my life as a project manager, I worked for multinational organizations. Most of them were not project-based organizations, I mean the level of importance and culture on project management was very low. I acted as a project manager but also as a project management discipline pioneer. I needed to preach about project management and to overcome all obstacles that appeared in my path. Getting invited and establishing internal relationships with other departments from my organizations was key for projects and organizational success.

Share Thoughts and Ideas

There are many benefits from sharing ideas at work (Figure 6.2). I thought it would be good to write this because I occasionally hear people talk about sharing creates stolen ideas and in return fighting over those stolen

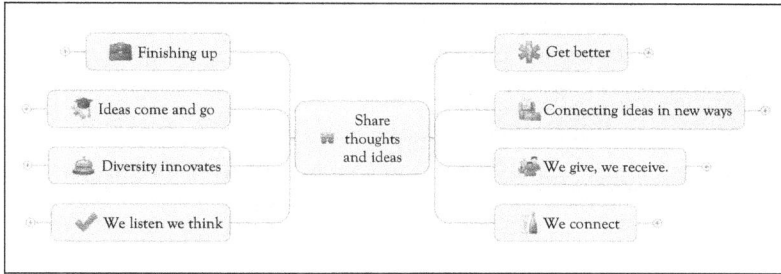

Figure 6.2 Share thoughts and ideas

ideas. There are other thoughts on why sharing ideas at work shouldn't be done but my focus on why it's a good idea is based on this opposition.

I don't know about you, but I want to work better. Not only do I want to work better, I want to get better at what I do every day. I have no desire to be the subject matter expert that holds my knowledge like a currency that people are trying to steal. Here are some of the reasons I like to share ideas at work and make what I know and learn public knowledge for others to benefit from:

1. *Get better*

   Every time I share ideas with others and have a discussion with them I get better. There's a natural exchange of ideas there and no single idea is original. By sharing ideas at work, I'm able to get better at my job while others also get better at their job. When I collaborate and share, everyone is improving at the same time, which then allows us all to reach higher levels of expertise even faster. I want to get better at my job and have more skills to transfer to other jobs if necessary and sharing does just that.

2. *Connecting ideas in new ways*

   One person can never have an idea that's perfect. By sharing my ideas at work, I am exposed to a side I may have never thought of before. New and better things come out of sharing ideas with others. Think about a subject matter expert who doesn't make their knowledge available to others unless forced and then it's a one-way road. They spew information as others record it.

This way of working never lets you connect your ideas with others and improve upon both ideas. There's no way one brain can think of every angle, so everybody has to cooperate and work together to reach a common larger goal. The human race is a cooperative race and it has allowed us to do great things. Sitting on an idea like you own it has never helped anybody meet a greater goal.

3. *We give, we receive*

By sharing ideas and working together, everyone involved benefits and receives a bit back. Without making it known what we're doing and thinking, it's impossible for others to contribute to that knowledge. The same goes for everyone else. If nobody makes it known what they're working on and what they're thinking, you won't be able to contribute to their work!

4. *We connect*

Modern work that isn't easy to automate is all based on connections. Connecting is uniquely human and can't be automated or taken away. The connections we make come through sharing knowledge and what we're working on in return allow us to do bigger things.

The more connections we make the more we can do in a shorter amount of time. Think about a project you've started and haven't known any of the people you're working on. That can be a challenge to get started figure out who is the best person for each job. If you have taken time to foster connections, then it's that much easier to find who you need to get things done.

5. *We listen, we think*

It's impossible to continue to spew information and ever learn anything from anybody. When we take a moment, shut up, and listen, we can gain a lot more insights and build on our own knowledge much easier.

Sharing ideas at work seems like it's the practice of just spewing information and never consuming, but it's not. Part of sharing your ideas and making that exchange of knowledge is in the consumption of others' ideas. As we read others' ideas and what they're working on, we have our own thoughts that we also share.

When we listen, we're forced to think about our own ideas and fine-tune those. If we listen, we're better equipped for the discussion with others to develop better ideas together.

6. *Diversity innovates*

The more minds that come together and from all different backgrounds, the better off we are able to come up with new and wonderful things. If everybody agrees on a solution and there was never any debating, there's a good chance that the solution won't be as good as it could have been. Diversity of thought allows for different angles of each idea to be uncovered. Great things come out of this.

7. *Ideas come and go*

Ideas are never something you want to hold like you own them, they aren't currency. Ideas are temporary and others will have the same ideas anyway. Connections are more important. Connecting with people and connecting of ideas. Connecting ideas is where innovation comes from and connecting with people makes those innovations come to life. Ideas aren't important to hold on to, and their only importance is in sharing them with others. Make yourself open and share with others what you're doing and what your thoughts are. Once you start doing this you'll find that the world begins opening up to you in new ways.

Expand beyond your organization's walls too. Never share only within your organization and never feel limited to the diversity it has to offer. The more you open up to the entire world and share with those across the globe, the more you'll learn and grow. Global connections introduce the diversity of ideas everyone needs. Ideas come and go but the diverse connections you can make globally cannot be replaced and will not fail you.

8. *Finishing up*

The idea for this book came from a very unlikely place that I would have never thought. Being open to reading those ideas and not just blowing them off is a great way to improve yourself. Amazing things happen when you inadvertently realize why you think what you think, and only others can help you reach those ideas.

Here's my finishing statement to sum it all up, the comment I made: When sharing happens, everyone is able to boost productivity at a faster pace. Also, more importance is put on problem-solving and innovation and not ideas that are impossible to hold for long. If you hold ideas as a currency for employment, then there will come a point when that currency is worthless. Value must be created and recreated in the form of the networks we create and maintain. That's not something that can be stolen, lost, or diminished.

Relationships Growing Tool

Networking is a relationship growing tool, but should you join just any network? Through my own research and interviews, I have seen that networks are only as valuable as those they bring together and what happens as a result (Figure 6.3). The innate value of a network and what you get out of it can make or break your chances for development. Before joining a network and putting in the energy to make it work, here are a few things to ask to make sure it's right for you:

Who is in the network? Network strength can be measured by the strength of the relationships between members and what each member brings to strengthen ties.

How well does the network connect? Increasing network strength requires both frequent and quality communication. Interactions that are consistent and demonstrate professionalism, integrity, respect, and confidence are essential to your own prospects. Quality interactions can happen anywhere, not only in the workplace. For example, one woman I interviewed described her networks like a spiderweb that drew many

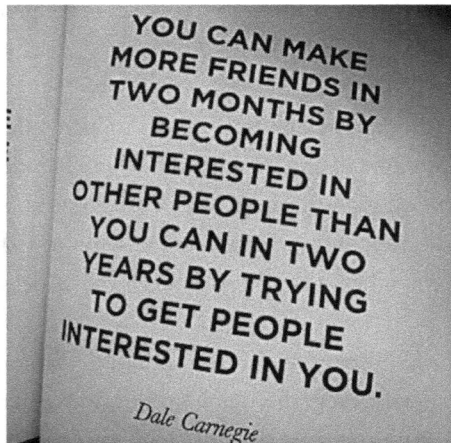

YOU CAN MAKE MORE FRIENDS IN TWO MONTHS BY BECOMING INTERESTED IN OTHER PEOPLE THAN YOU CAN IN TWO YEARS BY TRYING TO GET PEOPLE INTERESTED IN YOU.

Dale Carnegie

Figure 6.3 Your network

different people together. She described invitation-only reading groups that led to research collaborations, grant applications, and proposals for joint books.

These meetings and projects could entail a senior person working with someone more junior in a mentoring capacity. Joining a network that has professional associations means that the connections can share and enhance common goals, goodwill, commitment, and interests.

Is there functional communication? We all have days of frustration and disappointment at work. Being able to express these emotions can be a healthy way of letting off steam. If your network operates under an ethos of support, it means that your frustrations and disappointments will be heard in order to resolve problems, lend support, and provide assistance to overcome your frustrations and prevent burnout. Care and concern create network value because they are resources that help build trust and support. Ask yourself, does your network offer support that enables you to overcome difficulties?

Who are you talking to? Networking with more senior representatives has its benefits. Having access to a powerful spokesperson and building your connections is one way of working toward extending your network. For example, the golden skirts is an informal network supporting women on corporate boards. Members of the golden skirts, who are also members of other networks, are able to represent and speak on behalf of their other golden skirt members among a diverse range of other business, corporate, and education networks. They are almost twice as likely to be invited to other boards! Seek ways to represent your interests to those in other networks and to those more senior.

Your time is valuable and networking can be hit and miss if you cannot assess the value of your network first. Before you start networking, find out about the network and how it can help you move toward your goals.

What Else Do You Consider Before Joining a Network?

In our channel universe, we all know that professional relationships are critical to success and survival and that not all relationships are equal. Often, channel partners must navigate the tricky terrain of successfully managing both vendor and customer relationships. Sometimes, that's not an easy task. I find that savvy channel partners have the ability to keep successful and rewarding relationships with their vendors and, even more importantly, with their customers. Regardless of the method that you use to manage those relationships, the key is maintaining them at a high level of satisfaction.

Crossroads

At some point, you may come to a crossroads with a customer (Figure 6.4). How do you deal with customers who are high-maintenance, *but* you need their business? Or, maybe you're dealing with customers who are low-maintenance and easy to manage, but are low profit and may not be worth keeping?

Now and then, you may sit down with your team and talk about who to keep and who to cut. Unless you can net down the pros and cons, this can turn into a circular discussion that you keep having, with no results. I came across an interesting way to help you evaluate the value of your relationships to determine which ones are strategic and which ones serve only to suck time and resources out of your day and frustrate you.

Figure 6.4 Crossroads

The Matrix

The strategic relationship matrix is the brainchild of author and productivity guru Michael Hyatt. He was inspired to design it from the basis of the Boston Consulting Group's (BCG) growth-share matrix (Figure 6.5), which was developed in the late 1970s as a portfolio-planning model.

Just as a refresher, the BCG model is based on the rationale that a company's business units can be classified into four categories: dogs, question marks, stars, and cash cows. A classification is based on combinations of market growth and market share relative to the largest competitor, thus the name "growth share." I like Hyatt's strategic relationship matrix because he positions it as a way that you and your team can discuss and add analysis to in order to determine the value of the current relationships that you have with your customers. Are they easy and profitable, or are they draining and difficult to maintain? Up to what point do you keep the relationship, whether it's a customer or vendor?

Why Is Rating Customer (or Vendors) Important?

Time is finite and valuable, and you need to invest it where you're going to get the most return. By prioritizing your relationships, whether those are customers or vendors, you know where to aim your focus. Let's face

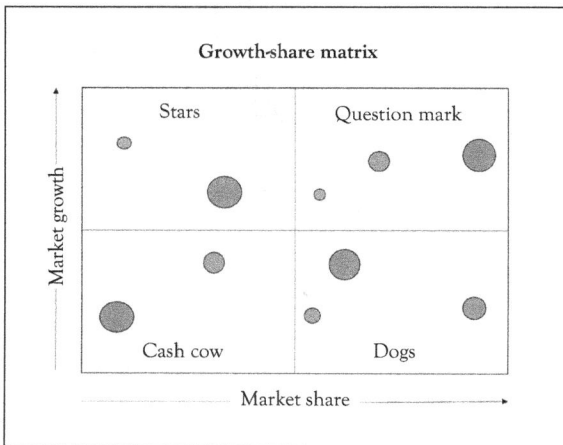

Figure 6.5 Adapted from Boston Consulting Group's growth-share matrix

Figure 6.6 Rating customer or vendor

it: We all have only so much time and budget, so prioritization is the key to effectiveness. Every professional relationship your organization has should have a level of maintenance assigned and a corresponding level of action associated (Figure 6.6).

As an example, the profile of a high-profit, low-maintenance relationship is one you certainly want to replicate with your prospective customers. What are their key attributes, and how can you find more like them?

Focus where you can reap the greatest benefit. It's that simple. You can use this to gauge the value of your vendor relationships, products that you carry, customer relationships, and more. There are only 24 hours in a day. Make the most of them.

Chapter Summary

From all ideas and concepts shared in this chapter, it is very important to remind you:

- As a project manager you need to work through people, so you need to grow up your relationships step by step.

- You need insight into what is the chemical substance that helps you to get a positive reaction among people. You can attract people.
- As a project manager you need to establish, maintain, and sustain relationships with your colleagues, peers, and other project stakeholders. One of my best practices is trying to be invited to other business meetings.
- Share your ideas and thoughts and share it with your colleagues, peers, and customers.
- Networking is a relationship growing tool, but you should not join just any network. You need to be selective.

References

Bucero, A. 2010. *Today is a Good Day: Attitudes for Achieving Project Success.* Ontario, Canada: Multimedia Publications.

Englund, R.L., and A. Bucero. 2012. "The Complete Project Manager: Building the Right Set of Skills for Greater Project Success." Paper presented at PMI® Global Congress 2012, EMEA, Marseille, France. Newtown Square, PA: Project Management Institute.

CHAPTER 7

Taking Care of Your Career

If you want to achieve great goals, never ask for permission. Plan for it and do it.

—Alfonso Bucero

I found that most of project managers are evaluated based on job performance. That means, organizations evaluate them on how successful they deliver projects in terms of the iron triangle. I mean everyone in the organization expects the project manager has consistently delivered his or her projects on time, scope, and cost. Yet, this is how we are still being evaluated in terms of how well we can perform as a project manager. But I believe it is not enough to evaluate the performance of project manager.

Many of us get into project management by accident or by job promotion, not by way of design. You may see yourself to end up being a project manager, rather than careful consideration and intentionally pursued. But what is the typical career path for a project manager?

What usually happens in organizations is that a technical specialist is progressing in his or her job and being technically efficient and productive, gaining many good technical skills. As soon as he or she is good doing that, become part of a project team for some time, acquire some leadership skills and are assigned as a junior project manager. But managers are not asking if they like project management or not, if they like dealing with people or not.

If that project manager is successful, he or she will be assigned as a project manager for a more difficult project, so will build more and more skills, then he will be ready for a more complex project.

Breaking the Cycle

Many project managers that I talk to have some project management plan for the projects they are managing (Figure 7.1). Only a few of them,

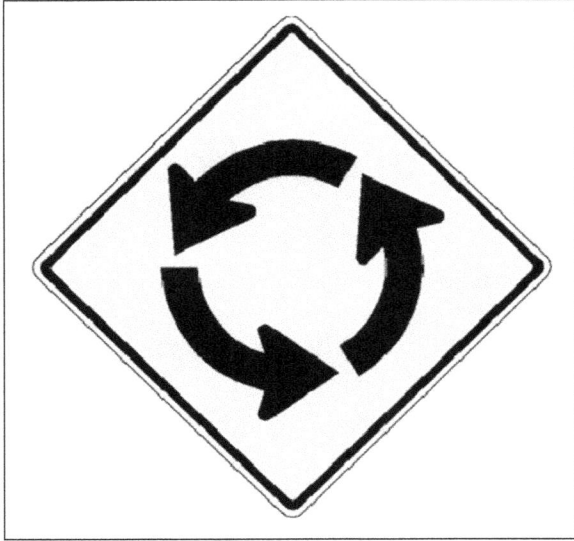

Figure 7.1 Breaking the cycle

however, would have any idea when I ask them, "Where is the project plan for your career?" As important as the projects that they are executing and managing, their career deserves to be written on paper with some high-level career goals, preferably some strategies or steps to follow to make it to the next level. In my experience, many project managers do not really know what the next level is.

They need to break the cycle and plan for his or her professional career. It takes time to reflect upon where you are and where you want to be. Starting with why is a very good start. Ask yourself the question, "Why am I a project manager?" and then ask you the "how" and finally you will obtain the "what's."

Plan for Your Career

If a project professional does not plan his or her professional career, no one will (Englund and Bucero 2012). This is my lesson learned over the years. Our career development is a project in itself and we need to take care of it very seriously, if want to progress professionally and personally. Then plan for your career. I will give you some clues about how to do it.

Identify Your Project Management Career Perspectives

Some professionals get lost at some point in their professional careers. Finding some help is needed in order to move forward and look for the right career movement (Figure 7.2).

Start by identifying several project manager career perspectives:

1. Organizational
2. Marketplace
3. Personal

Organizational

In any organization, there are two common threads that tie all the knowledge, processes, methods, tools, and solutions together in terms of how they serve the greater teams of people who go to work daily: ability and influence. Every individual has his specialty and ability to perform his job. Every professional has his circle of influence to affect how can do his job successfully as well as how his colleagues can do theirs. Each one of us must focus our career on how to influence the organization's

Figure 7.2 Professional career perspective

ability. Whether positive or negative, an organization is dependent on the collective ability of its professionals to fulfill their responsibilities with competency and professionalism. Anything short of that tall order could mean a negative impact to the organization's standing in the marketplace and how it is perceived as an employer. Particularly in the area of project management, developing a career path for professional project managers has been somewhat lacking and has not received the attention that is needed.

More and more project managers are finding that in order to leap across the career chasm, they may have to leave their current organization and get into leadership roles outside the project management realm, taking their collective wisdom and experience right along with them. I classify the employees of every organization in one of three areas: *doers, thinkers,* and *positive infectious.*

The *doers* are the ones who may be less experienced, still learning their jobs and learning why their job is critical to the operations of their department or team. Doers tend to focus on learning and supporting the business and helping to ensure relevance of their craft to the business processes, methods, and tools that are at their disposal. Doers can still have influence. It would be wise for leadership to make themselves available to the doers and gain insight on how their daily battles are won. Doers are the ones in the trenches delivering the results and are able to identify ways to help improve and demonstrate their value.

They need to find ways to connect with leaders of the organization and understand their needs, support their causes, and align their day-to-day activities to the strategies and goals that have been set at the organizational level. This is also a great way for the doers to give the leadership insight into the value they are delivering for the benefit of the organization. Influence does not flow in one direction. The doers can have just as much impact to the wellbeing of an organization as the decision makers at the top of the food chain.

The thinkers are the keepers of the gate. They are the ones that spend their time enhancing the way things are getting done, how to best implement project management methods and tools, and how to best communicate to the rest of the organization on how to deliver projects successfully.

They are the experts who know the ins and outs of all the organizations policies, processes—the "how's" of doing business. It is also their responsibility to approach the doers for ideas for improvements, enhancements, and identify future capabilities. They are also the ones who will take their time to decide whether an existing process or tool needs to be revamped or replaced by determining if their user base is readily adopting, vociferously rejecting, or finding alternative ways to do better and be better. It is to the *thinkers'* advantage to leverage these voices to identify ways to improve how projects are managed and how the organization can support their project managers.

The infectious is responsible for the ideation and proliferation of project management knowledge. The infectious has more experience and awareness of the organization's project management processes and the inner workings of various project organizations or departments across the organization. Their focus needs to be around maturing the organization—not just the PMO—but the entire organization. They need also focus on helping the *doers* and *thinkers* learn and contribute to the organization's PM capability. Ideas that are formulated by the *infectious* should be followed up with action plans and strategies to improve or to implement. Knowledge sharing is a must and it must be done readily across the organization.

Finally, the *infectious* need to encourage and facilitate innovation across the organization. The *infectious* need also know how to quantify and qualify success and pinpoint how the project management practice is contributing to those do your successes. Each project completed successfully should be leveraged to encourage learning, innovation, and knowledge sharing to maintain success and growth across the organization. Proliferation of the science and art of project management is highly dependent on an organization with a strong *infectious* group.

Marketplace

We live in a world in which change is inevitable. According to the Bureau of Labor Statistics, the average tenure of employment around the world has significantly decreased over the past 30 years. This change, however, does not necessarily need to cause any angst among project management professionals but rather an opportunity. This change also gave us a clear indication that our job is no longer about doing our job. If we cannot manage change in our professional career, then we could become extinct because someone else may be trying to get rid of our job from above or take our job from below. We have to be comfortable with change, which means we need to learn to deal with change.

The professional job market has taught us over the years that we are not hired to just occupy a desk or even to just perform a specific function. We are hired to deliver value, to improve our organization, to innovate, to share our knowledge, and to drive the changes that are necessary for the organization to remain competitive in today's world economy. Project management is the facilitator to making all these things happen and your project management career should be especially change-ready.

The modern job market is also teaching us that you can no longer spend a 45-year career doing one thing. What employers are looking for from perspective employees are no longer just technical skills, traditional business, or scientific acumen, but rather attitudes and willingness to learn and adapt.

The traditional career ladder that may offer fewer job changes, linear promotions, longevity in a single firm, and highly dependent on internal politics is being replaced by a career lattice that can offer many role changes, promotion by transitions (job changes), short sprints, and opportunities that are made available through extensive networking, both inside and outside the organization and sometimes even industry. Jobs are also becoming more nonlinear in that one person is expected to take on multiple roles, wear different hats, and do different things in this age of "do more with less" mentality.

One of the best things you bring to work every day is your attitude. Your attitude is revealed in the marketplace by the relevance of your knowledge and skills, how well you are connected with your network of peers, professional contacts, and leaders within your organization and your industry. Your attitude is also demonstrated through your competence; that is, demonstrating tangible business and operational results that you can point to as your past success. More importantly, you will need to be able to correlate your past successes to future benefit of the organization. And finally, your attitude is reflected by your eminence on your team, in your organization, in the industry, and in the professional community. Are you known in the workplace for your expertise, your professionalism, and your achievement? Are the leaders in your firm referring to you and your success as an asset to the organization? Are you willing and able to share those successes publicly? As a professional, humility is great, but invisibility is not.

Personal

Over the years, the job market has seen huge transformations to what the employers are looking for to how jobs are marketed and filled by HR organizations, staffing firms, and independent recruiters. The following statistics are very telling to how the job market has transformed its business practices as a result of the transition from the "career ladder" to the "career lattice."

- Eighty percent of job openings are not posted anywhere. Not in the newspaper, not on a job site, not even in most company's job postings. They remain between the ears of the hiring managers.
- On average, 118 people apply to a single job posting and only 20 out of those receive an interview.
- Fifty percent of résumés are weeded out by "talent management software" before a single human even looks at a single one.
- It takes a hiring manager just seven seconds of "eye time" to reject a résumé (Smith 2013).

The Résumé

The importance of a well-written résumé is obvious. With the amount of scrutiny that a résumé goes through in a job search process, it certainly deserves our utmost attention. However, most of us have never had any formal training in résumé writing. It is not until recently that colleges and universities began teaching résumé writing as part of a formal curriculum.

For most experienced project managers, they historically resort to borrowing and leveraging templates from colleagues, friends, family, and even online. Though not necessarily a bad thing, you have to remember that not all résumés are equal. In fact, not all of your own résumés are equal. Let me explain.

Most people have a single résumé that documents their entire working life. From the moment they stepped off the college campus until now. The résumé is inundated with job descriptions and experiences in a life. The problem with such a resume is that though it may contain what a recruiter or hiring manager is looking for, it also contains a whole lot of things that do not have any bearing to specific job requisition, leaving the hiring manager having to fish for information.

Your résumé should be meaningful. Meaning, the "stories" you choose to share should be relevant to the job you are applying for. This also means that you will have to craft the content of your resume to address the holes that the hiring manager is trying to fill. If every one of your experiences, and more importantly, who you are and how you have behaved in those experiences, demonstrates clearly an ability to address the most pressing needs of the hiring manager, you will have a much better chance of gaining at least an interview.

Remember, your résumé is about you. Not your previous job, not your previous teams. It is about how you have behaved on your job, with your team, through tough situations, delivering certain value and achieving certain results, and how such behavior in such context can achieve the desired results for which the hiring manager is searching. Your goal of writing a résumé is to get your point across, not your entire history. Quantity is not better than quality. So, when you write your résumé, consider these:

- Write in paragraph form.
- Write about your performance, not your job description.
- Highlight your career and how it is relevant to the person reading.

Highlight your experiences by using this simple technique that I would like to call the C.A.R. technique.

C—Circumstance

For each experience, start off by offering the context of your experience. What are the business problems that you were trying to solve or the business condition or problem statement that was given to you? What was the gravity of the situation? What are the pain points you are trying to alleviate? As a hiring manager, context is just as important as the characterization of you. If I told you I ran 26 miles, all you know was that I ran 26 miles. You do not know why I did it, how I did it, how long it took, or who was with me. Uphill? Downhill? I really do not know how good or bad of a runner you are. Your résumé needs to tell me who you are, how you have behaved, and the results you have achieved and you cannot do that without a setting.

A—Action

Once I know the gravity of the situation you were in, I want to know how you behaved. Now, this does not mean I want to know what you were tasked to do. I do not really want to know your job description. I want to know how, based on the context that you have just described, you have understood the problem or situation and behaved in the manner that demonstrated your ability to think creatively, to leverage your knowledge appropriately, to communicate broadly, to answer questions succinctly, to deal with animosity professionally, and to collaborate continually. Those are the qualities for which, above all of your credentials and accolades, most hiring managers are looking.

R—Result

This is the part that most people leave out on their résumé. What were the end results? Did you save your organization from needless spending? Did your team avoid certain risks that would have been otherwise unavoidable? What were the tangible benefits realized or improvements achieved that can be directly or even indirectly attributed to your actions? It is not a good story unless you know what happens in the end, so do not leave out the ending to yours!

The Interview

There are so many about how to prepare and do an interview. I will simply remind you of what we have been discussing previously. Your entire job search process is about you as a person, as a worker, and as an employee. Your interviewers will be less concerned about your credentials and your skills than who you are and how you have behaved in your previous professional environments and endeavors.

Your job at the interview is to bring your attitude, which, as we had previously discussed, is demonstrated by the relevance of your skills, your competence that leads to future benefits, your professional connections, and your eminence in the industry. Be a storyteller at the interview and let yourself be the main character. And, remember, the story is about its main character, not about job description or team.

I Already Have a Job

If you already have a job, congratulations. However, we live and work in a very tough and competitive business environment. Someone above could be looking to get rid of your job and someone below you could be looking to take over your job. Having a job is great, but having a career is better. And in order to achieve a successful career, you have to be mindful of the way "jobs" fit into a modern career. In order for you to ditch the "career ladder" and embrace the "career lattice," you always have to be on the lookout for your next "job."

Now, looking out for your next job does not mean that you need to apply for new jobs every day. Looking out for your next job means that, every day, you are doing something to prepare yourself to be successful at your next opportunity, whether this next job is with your current organization or not. Reflect on the questions given as follows:

- What are my unique skills and abilities today?
- How marketable are my skills and abilities?
- What skills and abilities do I want to acquire tomorrow?
- What do I enjoy doing today?
- What do I want to pursue tomorrow?

- How can I differentiate myself from others?
- What am I worth in the market? Why?
- What value do I add to my employer, customer, and industry?

You need to be, in fact, constantly thinking about your personal brand. Your personal brand is your unique promise of value. It is composed of your business expertise and its viability in the marketplace. If you are still holding on to 50-year-old technology and methodology that has not been updated or improved, your expertise may not be as marketable in this fiercely competitive job market. Your brand is also about how you are uniquely known in the marketplace. Do you create value? How do you create value? What character defines you? What are your principles? What will make your brand great will be based on how integral your behavior is to your craft, whether it can be clearly understood and whether it is compelling. Your brand showcases your passion about what you do and subsequently demonstrated by your behavior. This is what will differentiate you from others. A great brand indicates future value, substantiated by past relevant success and well-articulated with confidence and executive presence.

Every Job Is an Audition

You are either auditioning to your current boss or a potential future boss. The term we like to use for auditioning to your current boss is *promotion*. However, our tradition may have led us into some very unrealistic attitudes toward promotion. We tend to think in terms of the organizational structure and job titles when we should think in terms of ability and influence (remember those?). True promotion is about your ability to influence backed by your experience.

True promotion cannot be easily taken away from you because influence is not guaranteed by a job title. It is by your dedication and effort to your work, your ability to visibly demonstrate your competence, and how well you are connected in the workplace. A title may be a manifestation of someone else's recognition of your influence, but by then, it is just icing on the cake.

Building Your Network

Having a good professional network does not make you the "teacher's pet." Having a good professional network means you have demonstrated professional competence and that you are known in the marketplace for your knowledge, dedication, and ability to communicate. Having a good network can provide you with the exposure to the right experience to allow you to demonstrate your ability and increase your reach in the marketplace. Your network can also help you stay relevant because you connect to others who are just like you—they too can demonstrate their abilities—and learning from other professionals about what is viable in their profession is never a bad thing (Bucero 2010).

If you have not already, it is critical that you begin building your network by identifying those who can be your mentors. You need to learn from those who have been where you are and where you are headed. Learn from their mistakes and failures and how they recovered from those mistakes and failures to achieve results. Mentors can also find opportunities for you to shine and provide insight to how you can personally and professionally improve to maintain the proper "attitude" (in the sense that we have previously discussed).

At the same time, be a mentor. Find someone who is more junior than you and share your experiences and your past mistakes and failures and how you have recovered and succeeded. Find opportunities for them to shine. If you are worried about "grooming someone to replace you," do not. I have never seen someone losing her job for being a good mentor.

Be Knowledgeable About The Job Market

Do you know what career options you have and where to find jobs in these career sectors? Different careers require different approaches: Some employers look for relevant qualifications for example, postdoctoral positions require a PhD; some specialist environmental or business companies look for applicants with a master's degree; some employers want applicants to demonstrate relevant skills and experience through previous paid or voluntary work; others have to annual graduate training programs with set deadlines for applications.

Some other people do not care about titles or credentials, and they are looking for experts. Credentials are important for them but the most weight is placed on the experiences the candidate had and how he or she dealt with issues, risks/opportunities, and issues.

Monitor Your Progress

You need to monitor your progress periodically. Your professional environment is in constant change, so you need to be ready for the change. We are now in the era of do-it-yourself career development. Companies less frequently offer formal training—a trend that has been around for years. This may be because employees change jobs so frequently (job tenure now averages about four years) that firms don't see the value in investing in people who are likely to leave. This is a sharp contrast to the investment that senior leaders used to make in employees. During my almost 14 years at Hewlett-Packard, mostly during the 1990s, "personal development" was treated as a major company initiative.

Unfortunately, organizations today are unknowingly leaving employees with skill gaps and blind spots that can derail careers and organizational effectiveness. And managers are not helping. Too worried about their own hides, most managers do not have time or energy to focus on anyone else's.

Ideally, organizations would do more to foster career development: encourage more-immediate feedback, develop clear performance criteria, deliver developmental feedback with clarity and tact, and provide resources and incentives for managers to make employee development a priority. But the reality is that the bigger burden is on employees. Workers at all levels must learn to identify their weaknesses, uncover their blind spots, and strengthen their skills. Here are six things you can do to take control of your career development:

1. *Understand what you are evaluated on*: What does success look like in your position? What are your job goals and success metrics? It's best to identify these with your manager, but if that's not happening, then write down what you understand the goals and key performance

indicators to be. Take them to your boss to get their agreement and engage in an ongoing dialogue to ensure you stay on the right track.

2. *Solve for your own blind spots*: Top performers are always learning and adjusting, and routinely seek feedback from their boss, peers, and subordinates. If your boss doesn't proactively give you feedback, start the conversation yourself. After a presentation or big meeting, state one thing that you think went well, and then ask for advice on one thing you could improve. It's best to keep it simple; most people can only absorb one area to improve at a time. Listen to and thank your boss for the feedback.

3. *Codify your learnings*: You can capture feedback and learning by keeping a journal. List the five to ten skills or competencies you need to develop in your position, and rate yourself (either on your own or with the help of a trusted adviser) on each. For example, if you're a brand marketer, you might give yourself an A in advertising development, a B+ in pricing analysis, and a C in trade marketing. Focus on the C's to close skill gaps. Seeking feedback from someone who previously held your job can speed up your learning.

4. *Increase your visibility with senior leaders*: It is not always possible to get noticed by senior leaders through your direct work, so you might try volunteering for initiatives, such as charity work, company events, or on-campus recruiting. This is an easy but often overlooked way to rub shoulders with senior people who will see you in action and ideally take notice of your contributions.

5. *Become an expert in an area of increasing importance to your company*: Your company may be grappling with a disruption from a new technology such as the Internet of Things, artificial intelligence, or Cloud-based computing. Become the expert person in your department on an emerging issue. Conduct research and literature reviews, attend conferences, or write on the topic. Developing expertise in a nascent area of growing importance can lead to promotions and other career opportunities.

6. *Seek good counsel and mentoring*: The perspective of a senior person is invaluable but pouncing on someone to ask, "Will you be my mentor?" is likely to scare them off. Try to meet in an informal way: in the coffee shop in your company's lobby, or at the company picnic

or golf outing. Know the person's bio and be prepared to ask a few good questions related to their area of expertise. If things go well, you'll hear, "If I can help you, let me know." A week or so later, you can extend an invitation to "continue the conversation" over coffee. In time, a mentor relationship may develop organically.

Work on Your Purpose and Vision

I found several definitions of purpose: the reason for which something exists or is done, made, or used; an intended or desired result, end, aim, or goal. Other definitions are determination and resoluteness. I believe that every one of us has a purpose. For example, my purpose is "to help organizations to change their attitude to manage more successful projects." Think about your purpose.

For some people it is not easy to find their purpose but my advice is there to reflect on. It takes a while but is worth. When you discover your purpose, please write it in a document and be committed to pursue it. Remember that you can do it because you are excellent. Identifying your purpose will help you to work on your vision. In the book *The Complete Project Manager* (coauthored with Randall L. Englund), we explain that the vision consists in a vivid description of your future situation. There are four basic characteristics that a vision needs to have: clear, concise, convincing, and compelling. Work on your vision for some time.

For example, my vision is:

We have a PM services organization which effectively consults, trains, coaches and helps customers on managing projects, programs and portfolios by providing customized and professional solutions to maintain and sustain a positive attitude for organizational success.

Professional Career Assessment Tool

I have put together an extensive guide to serve as a beginning point and reference for your future career as a project manager. You can now start being part of this line of work right away by reading the basics of each aspect of a project manager's career growth.

Here are the things that you should consider before starting a project management career:

1. What does be a project manager actually mean?
2. A project manager's skills
3. What does a project manager actually do?
4. What is the secret of a project management career?
5. How to become a project manager?
6. Education
7. Income

What Does Being a Project Manager Actually Mean?

Are you always the leader of your group who likes to keep everything and everyone organized and with a goal in mind?

If your answer is yes, you could be on your way to a career in project management. Project management is one of the most complex fields of work out there. Be prepared for a true adventure you'll never get bored of. There is no space for dullness in this profession. A project manager is responsible for leading an entire project through initiation, planning, execution, control, and completion.

Project managers always work in a team. They are most often sociable and great team players. As a project manager, you will need to adapt to different people, cultures, environments, and situations. Being flexible is key to team communication since you'll be the builder and controller of the team.

To be a great project manager, you have to be a team leader, coworker, and supervisor at the same time. This is one of the most challenging careers as no day will be the same and you will need all of your skills to solve every problem. Also, you'll be the first person your team goes to when a problem occurs. They might expect you to hold the answers to any inquiry. But, this is what makes the project management career interesting.

You will deal with both formal and informal interactions. If you believe that you're a person who knows people well from the second you meet them, this might be the right career path for you. Essentially, the project manager is similar to a psychologist. They know exactly what problems, desires, and expectations employees and clients have. However, despite being a people person, a project manager won't get emotionally involved in their projects. Some of your duties will include: taking part in the creation process, executing the project, preparing communication methods, finding solutions to recurring issues, monitoring the project's progress from start to finish, and many more. To put it briefly, you'll be responsible for connecting each project to the business world and to its clients.

You must be aware that the entire responsibility of the project's success will fall on your shoulders. You will be held accountable for any mistakes that your team makes or for any client complaints. In this position, you'll focus both on the accuracy of your work and that of your team.

This profession is always changing and facing new demands. If you're the kind of person who prefers diversity, this is the type of career you'll never get bored of. You can always switch the project you're working on, the team you interact with, the industry you're involved in, and even the processes and tools to ease your work. No project is the same. Yet, your expertise in this field will prove helpful whenever you'll come across similar situations and issues in the future. Similarly, your past experience will be essential to solving problems quickly.

A Project Manager's Skills

Knowledge of project management is sometimes just not enough for you to become a great project manager. As discussed earlier, you need soft skills as well. Being a good communicator and an open leader is not enough. Tackling daily project management challenges also requires accountability, adaptability, analytical and strategic thinking, decisiveness, a stress-resistant personality, and even a bit of love for risk-taking. Being a multitasker with great written and oral communication skills can place you among the top project managers in your sector.

When it comes to hard skills, you should be aware that there is no specific project management skill. In fact, depending on the project, you'll have to know a bit of everything. General business knowledge is highly desired. Don't worry though, you don't need to be an expert in technical skills such as coding. However, being able to give accurate and detailed tasks to your developers is important. Leading a project is all about making sure that your team members lack no information that's crucial to successfully finish a task and delivering the final project.

You should have the adequate level of knowledge to spot an issue and suggest possible solutions. At the same time, you should know that many project managers have had previous other jobs such as software developers, marketing managers, accountants, designers, and so on. This means that they hold the required solid knowledge for projects related to their previous fields of interest. If you're one of these people, you might be one step ahead of the others; but you must keep in mind that you'll also need to develop your own knowledge of project management processes, frameworks, and people management. You might be used to working individually, but project management is all about teamwork. Don't panic if you end up realizing that working as a project manager is not a right fit for you. This profession creates many new opportunities and pathways for other future careers.

Take a look at the skills of the most successful project managers and find out if you have what it takes to become like them and what you have to improve:

- Solid understanding of business cases and risk management processes
- Expert knowledge to meet specific circumstances
- Proven project management and self-management skills
- Strong leadership skills
- Ability to monitor and control budgets
- Critical thinking
- Good communication and negotiation skills
- Capability to make decisions under pressure
- Strong interpersonal skills necessary to lead a team
- Ability to define situations, document data, and draw conclusions
- Strong business acumen
- Ability to interpret instructions regardless of their form
- Strong organizational and multitasking skills

- Creative mindset
- Analytical skills
- Accuracy and attention to detail
- Excellent time management skill
- Capacity to maintain schedules and meet deadlines
- Problem-solving skills
- Self-motivation
- Accountability
- Working knowledge of project management tools

What Does a Project Manager Actually Do?

Depending on the industry you work in, your duties might differ. I analyzed over 200 LinkedIn worldwide job postings and compiled this list of the most common project manager responsibilities:

- Direct all project management phases
- Set and manage project expectations with external and internal stakeholders
- Coordinate and track various projects through an entire project lifecycle
- Develop a detailed project plan to track project progress
- Mentor, motivate, and supervise project team members
- Develop professional business relationships
- Define the overall scope of the project
- Prioritize the tasks of the project
- Create and continuously update the project documentation
- Create accurate forecasts for revenue and resource requirements
- Partner with all departments to ensure work is done according to demands
- Establish effective communication
- Ensure team members have all the necessary information
- Track work times and maintain accurate daily time sheets
- Ensure project tasks are executed and reviewed within the predefined scope

- Align various teams to maintain the quality of deliverables
- Report and escalate issues to management when necessary
- Conduct project status meetings, daily standups, and retrospective meetings
- Continuously follow up on the progress, risks, and opportunities of the project
- Focus on customer satisfaction
- Manage projects through key performance indicators (KPIs)
- Manage budgets and billings
- Act as the main customer contact for project activities
- Make recommendations for project improvements
- Conduct workshops and trainings
- Obtain customer input
- Measure project performance using appropriate systems, tools, and techniques
- Evaluate team performance

What's the Secret of a Project Management Career?

There is no definite secret. Project managers are good at their job for various reasons. Thinking that you hold the secrets of this job can make you believe that you're prepared for any situation. Nevertheless, there are many problems that could occur anytime, making it impossible for you to know how to solve them without too much struggle. For this reason, it is better to focus on being a great professional rather than on hunting down the secrets of success. Doing what the best PMs are doing won't guarantee that you'll become successful like them.

Being passionate and open to change whenever something is not working right though is more important. The project management world is one of the most dynamic business environments. You should be able to adapt to its changing nature and become comfortable in it.

Another tip that project managers might hesitate to share has to do with the use of project management tools. These can automate their tasks and help them manage projects with ease. Finding the perfect tools often takes a lot of time and testing. Also, the apps and techniques you'll use can depend on your style of work.

More experienced project managers might even be able to tell you some secrets that you'll find nowhere else. The true secrets of this profession come only with experience. Making mistakes and learning from them is a valid statement even in project management.

Meanwhile, some of the things that you can test are: making sure that you understand the client's requirements, picking the right team members, being able to create tasks in detail, making sure you have the best tools and systems for finishing the project, focusing on the real issues, setting reasonable requirements, always taking failure into consideration, and creating backup plans.

Do not forget: Testing methods and tools is vital for the project success and for your development as a professional. By testing and experimenting, you'll be able to learn the secrets of project management on your own. This is beneficial since the tips you'll get from another project manager might not apply to your project. You must be aware that every PM is different and every project is peculiar in its own way.

How to Become a Project Manager

Where should you actually start your education to become a project manager?

Before you begin your project management journey, you have to see if this career is right for you. Read the stories of other project managers, reach out to them, ask questions, or try a project management internship. Additionally, you can take some introductory online courses to get your first look at this subject. Usually, these courses provide tasks and assignments designed to make you interact with this business branch and see if you can handle its responsibilities.

Remember this: You should never start working as a project manager without having previously discovered the processes and tools commonly used in project management. You have to know if you're capable of using those techniques and platforms before you take part in a real project.

Before you start looking for a job, write down all of the aspects that your future workplace must have and make a list of what you never want to deal with in your following career. Don't rush into getting a job just for the sake of working. If you're at the beginning of your career, you should find a work environment that allows you to grow and learn more from your coworkers.

This takes us to the importance of having a mentor. We've previously talked about how you could research the activity of other project managers before deciding whether this path is right for you or not. A role model can shape your entire career. This is the reason why you should find a skilled project manager who'd be able to allocate part of his time to teach you what he already knows. By working close to their side, you'll master project management methods, methodologies, frameworks, processes, and best practices. A mentor's purpose is also to honestly highlight your mistakes so that you can use them to further develop yourself.

Know that finding compatible project managers who want to share their wisdom and knowledge can be rather difficult. Most, however, will be willing to do this in return for some help with their tasks. As a result, they'll involve you in real projects and even supervise you while doing so. This is imperative for a project management novice because you wouldn't otherwise be able to know if you're using your theoretical knowledge correctly without someone analyzing your work. Trust is at the base of the trainee–mentor relationship. You believe they'll share their tips with you and they allow you to work on projects with them.

Education

Your project management career can start with you getting a project manager or business administration degree. Not having a diploma in project management is, however, not a disadvantage; but, if you do study it on a daily basis in an academic environment, you'll have a head start. It's never too late to switch to a career that suits your interests. In fact, project management does not belong to only one industry. Usually, projects will belong to another line of business such as software, art, logistics, economics, linguistics, and so on. In fact, a design agency might require you to hold a degree in arts or design for a better understanding of the field. In this case, project management education is entirely up to your own will and desire to improve yourself professionally.

Any college degree can prove helpful for a future project manager since the academic world teaches you how to study and acquire knowledge gradually. This is essential for a project manager that could have to learn all about a new project's main field in a short time. Self-development, self-learning, and a will to constantly develop oneself throughout a lifetime are vital for keeping your career at the top.

Before deciding on a degree, see how project management works in real life. College activities do not allow you to see the actual consequences of your decisions. Working with a real project can teach you all about accountability and outcome management.

There are also numerous online project management learning resources, blogs, and programs that you can follow. This could be an option if you don't live close to the college you'd like to attend or if you just don't have enough time to attend university.

Another way of educating yourself is getting a similar position. You don't have to begin your career as a PM. You can start from managing smaller projects, products, or even teams. Alternatively, you can go for an internship in this field. Don't get discouraged if the work you'll be doing won't seem like something you'll love for the rest of your life. Sometimes all it takes is to find a different project to work on. All project managers dream of working in a field that is actually one of their hobbies. If your hobby is in the field of business, you're lucky.

Project Management Certifications

Are project management certificates still worth it? Of course! As you advance in your career you will either feel the need to certify your project management knowledge or you will be asked by your employer to get a certificate. Although certificates might slowly start losing their importance for recruiters, the experience you'll get during trainings and exams is indispensable.

Having a project management certificate is a plus, but extensive knowledge and experience in the field matter more for a project's success. What you must remember is that certificates are not everything. You could have all the diplomas in the world and, yet, if you have no real knowledge or working experience in project management, no one will want to work with you.

Which are the Most Important PM Certificates Out There?

Do not rush into studying for just any project management certification. Some employers don't even accept them while online certifications are almost useless. Also, you should study for a certification that's related to the projects you work on or industry you're involved in.

Income

I always say that I am lucky because I love my profession, but you also need to earn money to make a life. Income is one key thing to think about. Project managers are well paid in general, but it also depends on the industry.

My suggestion is to belong to a professional association like Project Management Institute (PMI) who can give you some clues on project management jobs and salaries. They do some surveys every year with so accurate information on that subject and the survey results are usually published on some of their professional magazines. On the other hand, join a project management professional association and you will have the opportunity to ask questions to other peers and colleagues.

Finally, read business newspapers and business magazines where project management jobs are announced and you will learn in more detail what the market is looking for. Change is also present in market job demands, so learn from it and acquire the habit of reading periodically that type of information and reports.

Chapter Summary

If you want to be successful on your professional career, you need to plan for it. The following are important key points to remind about your professional career:

- Most organizations promote good technical people to the project management job without asking them if they want it.

- Project managers need to break the cycle and plan for his or her professional career. Our career development is a project itself and we need to take care of it very seriously, if want to progress professionally and personally.
- Every organization can place its employees in one of three areas: doers, thinkers, and positive infectious. Who are you?
- The importance of a well-written résumé is obvious.
- Your interviewers will be less concerned about your credentials and your skills than who you are and how you have behaved in your previous professional environments and endeavors.
- True promotion cannot be easily taken away from you because influence is not guaranteed by a job title.
- Having a good professional network means you have demonstrated professional competence.
- You need to monitor your progress periodically.
- Work on you purpose and vision.
- Assess your career (meaning, skills, characteristics, secrets, education and income.

References

Bucero, A. 2010. *Today Is a Good Day: Attitudes for Achieving Project Success.* Ontario Canada: Multimedia Publications.

Englund, R.L., and A. Bucero. 2012. "The Complete Project Manager: Building the Right Set of Skills for Greater Project Success." Paper Presented at PMI® Global Congress 2012, EMEA, Marseille, France. Newtown Square, PA: Project Management Institute.

CHAPTER 8

Using Your Courage

Success is not final, failure is not fatal. It is the courage to continue that counts.

—Winston Churchill

Courage is not the lack of fear (Figure 8.1), or the absence of fear is just to move forward even when you do not feel totally ready to do something new (Bucero 2010). Preparation is key for professional success but if you have an opportunity to try something new, please try it. I am a dreamer and I use my courage in my professional life to convert my dreams into reality. All of us had fear at times when trying new and challenging things but my advice is to move forward and try it. What happens if you fail? I usually apologize and try to learn more about the reasons of my failure.

One of my examples of applying courage was for the founding of the first PMI chapter in Spain. I was a project manager who worked for Hewlett Packard. Having some years of experience, I did not feel like a champion or the best project manager, but when I attended my first project management symposium in the United States in 1992, I did not understand why I was the only Spanish project manager there. Then and I said to myself: Alfonso, you need to propose to PMI for starting a PMI chapter in Spain. I was sure that we had a lot of project management practitioners in my country but they did not show up in that symposium. Many of them did not speak good English including me, and I moved forward.

As soon as I came back to Spain, I contacted several project professionals who were interested in my idea, and I tried to motivate them to move forward. I needed to contact PMI, even with my poor English level, but I used my passion, persistence, and patience and I did. It took some teleconferences and several face-to-face meetings. In fact, we organized our first project management professional event in Madrid. We made the

Figure 8.1 Courage

effort of creating a PMI chapter several times, and we found several obstacles. For example, not all the members of the team were committed to
dedicate some time periodically to work on the project plan preparation.
The first leader who started the initiative felt bad because he thought he
was not respected because of his race—he was African American. The
second leader tried to make more professionals interested, but he was
not very influential and did not succeed. We failed two times and turned
successful the third time. Finally, the PMI Madrid Chapter was formally
created in 2003, and I was one of the founders. I tried to collaborate as a
founder with the chapter's board of directors and I found some obstacles
again because of the personality of the first president. I decided to start
another PMI chapter in Barcelona because I have some good friends and
professionals there. And I did it two years later using my lessons learned
creating the Madrid chapter.

How Courage Can Help You to Develop the 3 Ps

Have good courage and prosperity will come. As a consequence, then you
shall have good success. In order to succeed in any profession, you have

to have good courage. It is related to self-confidence and that is a consequence of hard work on preparing yourself. In my experience, most of people who are well prepared are usually becoming self-confident persons.

In my case, as a believer, I say thank you God every day and he is all time with me. Then for fear, I do not feel alone. If you are not a believer, you can talk to yourself and say, "I can do it" and the only thing you need is to believe that you can. Gaining your self-confidence is key to apply your courage.

I remember that by the end of last year, I got discouraged and could not see much fruit of my business work. One of my project management colleagues asked me about my business progress by e-mail and told him about my discouragement because most organizations have changed the way they support people in project management. And one morning, as I was in my office, my colleague phoned me and wanted to know what I was discouraged about. I told him, because I could see no result from my work on my business, I did an special effort to create some new products and services and I could not sell them to my customers. He asked me a powerful question that I will never forget. That question was: Alfonso, are you committed to continue with your project management consulting business and dealing with it as a high priority? My answer was yes, definitely. He told me, "Ok then, never give up." If you are unhappy with the customers responses you got, change your strategy. I can help you to find other potential deals where you can move forward and present a proposal. Then a new window was opened for me. He made my day!

On one side, it was risky to move to other business sectors, new experiences, new customer contacts, and new environment, but I had the passion to continue with my business and also the support from my colleague, who has a lot of customer contacts. I had spent almost three years working on my new products and services. Then I used my persistence, and with my colleague's support, I started to find other potential customers to contact and sell my project management services. It took me close to three months, but I found some new customers and met some of them. Now I have been working since last January and in less than six months my progress was very good. I found some new customers interested in my project management services and have presented new proposals.

This is a real example about how my courage has helped me on my business continuity and how cultivating my three Ps (passion, persistence, and patience) are still helping me to continue. Develop your courage is possible and it is a consequence of practicing my three Ps and self-confidence. You can do it, remember that you are excellent, and then act as if you wear a crown in your head.

Some Obstacles About Courage

In 2006, I decided to start a Leadership Master Class from PMI (Figure 8.2). I have been a PMI volunteer over the years and I submitted my application to participate in that program. That Master Class was one year long and it was a blended training (face-to-face plus virtual classes and coaching). I started in May 2006 and I was studying and attending the training for six months, but suddenly my mother had an accident and she had a surgery on her left leg. Because of that I could not attend the second face-to-face session, so I lost a four-day class. But instead of giving up, I wrote a message to the Master Class coordinator and I told him that I wanted to continue, asking him what I could do to move forward. I needed to study in my own for a couple of months, and after being persistent with my request, I was accepted for another class two months later.

My courage was maintained because I used my persistence dealing with that issue and was patient in waiting an answer from PMI. It was great because at the end of the Master Class, when I was graduated, I had double amount of contacts from the first class and from the second one. In this case, my obstacle created an opportunity for me meeting and establishing a relationship with more colleagues.

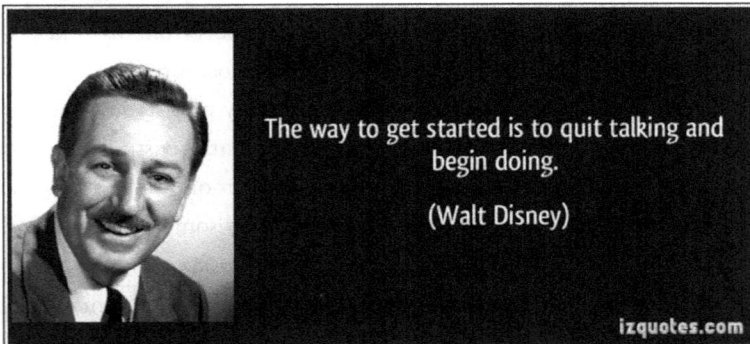

The way to get started is to quit talking and begin doing.

(Walt Disney)

izquotes.com

Figure 8.2 Some obstacles about courage

The greatest leaders do not just move past an obstacle—they find meaning in it and use it to their advantage. When you face a challenge, you cannot just look at how it is limiting you; you have to look at how it changes you, and how it could change you for the better. "Just as we develop our physical muscles through overcoming opposition—such as lifting weights—we develop our character muscles by overcoming challenges and adversity," said Stephen Covey.

All leaders eventually face hardship. Great leaders overcome those hardships and improve themselves in the process. Whether you are a boss, an entrepreneur, a scientist, or a mentor, you have to look at your weakest moments as opportunities rather than limitations. Every obstacle and every failure is just another step toward your ultimate destination: success.

Develop Your Courage

Courage is a personality trait that everyone possesses, but it sometimes falters because of bad experiences or memories (Figure 8.3). Having courage is necessary to succeed in many situations in life from meeting the opposite sex to doing your job. But by identifying the source of any lack of courage and actively changing your behaviors, you can build confidence in any aspect of your life.

Some suggestions are as follows:

1. *Determine your specific fears.* People are often reluctant to admit that they are afraid of something and this may be undermining their confidence and courage.

Figure 8.3 Develop your courage

- In order to begin building courage, you need to determine your specific fear. You may not even be aware of your specific fear(s) until you begin to think about what causes you to lack courage.
- Write a list of your fears as you figure them out. This may help you to develop a plan to overcome them and build your courage.
- This will likely not be an easy exercise because it often causes a person to feel embarrassed or ashamed.

2. *Figure out the cause of your fears.* The lack of courage, or timidity, often stems from some form of fear that is learned through experience or memory. Identifying the sources of your specific fears can help you to begin taking proactive steps to change this behavior and ultimately gain courage in any situation.

- Thinking about specific experiences that may have contributed to your lack of confidence and countering them with positive experiences can help to get you in the proper frame of mind to start building your confidence and courage. For example, perhaps you fear rejection by the opposite sex because someone rejected you once before. To offset this fear, think about situations where the opposite sex has welcomed you.
- If you cannot identify a specific experience that is the source of your fear, it may be from a memory or a social fear, such as the shame of failure. For example, if you've never touched a snake, but are afraid of them, this may stem from someone related to you either telling you that snakes are dangerous. You can offset memory fears by actively thinking about when and how these fears may have been realized in the past.
- Thinking about your fears and their sources can help you to grow out of them over time. Simply acknowledging your fears may be the only thing you need to overcome them.

3. *Recognize your courage.* Just as it's important to identify your fears, you should also recognize that you also possess courage in many situations. Taking the time to acknowledge that you are courageous can help you to figure out how to apply this quality to situations in your life that cause timidity.

- Everyone possesses courage in some way, even if it's "hidden" or seemingly simple. For example, you may be open to moving often to other parts of your country or world, which requires courage not only to start over in new situations but also to take the risk of possible failure.
- Recognizing your courage can help you to develop your behavior and begin building courage in every aspect of your life.

4. *Develop a concrete plan to build your courage.* Once you've identified your specific fears and recognized situations where you exhibit courage, develop a concrete plan to work on building your courage. An explicit strategy you can follow may help you stay on track if you have setbacks or see your progress over time.

- Write out your plan and update it as necessary. Having a tangible list can help motivate you.
- For example, if you are afraid of driving alone on a highway, you can develop a plan to help you get used to it until you have the courage to take on the task. Your plan might include the items "ride in the passenger seat on the highway, drive with a friend or family member on major roads, drive alone on major roads, drive with a friend or family member on a highway, drive alone on the highway."

Develop Behaviors to Develop Courage

Every professional can develop some behaviors to develop his or her courage. Some lessons learned as a project professional helped me to suggest the following:

1. *Script situations that elicit your fears.* Tackling a fear can cause any person to lose confidence and avoid a situation that could otherwise help them build confidence. Employing the behavioral tactic of scripting can help you engage with otherwise scary situations and build courage.

- Scripting is a technique where you conceptualize a game plan or "script" for a specific situation and follow through with it.

For example, if you are scared of speaking to your boss, write notes and develop a plan that will allow you to have equal command of the meeting. Think about what you could say in response to any questions or contingencies that may arise in your interaction.

2. *Frame what you fear in simpler terms.* If you are confronted with something that causes you fear or to lose courage, frame it in simple terms. Framing is a behavioral technique that can help you shape how you think and feel about specific situations by making them seem commonplace or banal.

   • For example, if you are afraid to swim in the ocean, you can reframe it as "this is just a very large pool and I will stay within this specific area."

   • Working with smaller and more manageable units of anything will help build your courage.

3. *Avoid comparing yourself to others.* Every person is different and comparing yourself to other people can minimize your self-confidence. Focusing on yourself and not comparing yourself to others is essential to building your confidence and courage.

   • Keep in mind that while some people may possess courage in some situations, you likely possess it that others may not. If you get into a situation with someone who has courage in a situation that you don't, for example if fellow teammate never seems to worry about letting others down and you do, think about something that you excel at that they don't. Shifting the focus back to your ability can help you to see that you have courage.

   • Many people may project courage in order to intimidate others. Don't let another person's courage or confidence undermine yours.

4. *Embrace the positive and avoid the negative.* Negative thoughts and attitudes are draining and if you give in to them, they will become stronger and undermine your confidence and courage. Seeking out the positive in any situation will help build your overall courage.

   • Even in the most fearful situations, there is always some aspect of courage. It might take some time to recognize but being able to see these courageous aspects in anything will help build your confidence and courage.

5. *Have confidence and believe in your ability to be courageous.* Two characteristics of a courageous person is that they not only have confidence in themselves, but also that they believe in their ability to succeed and overcome fears [16]. By cultivating and projecting confidence in yourself and to others, you set yourself on the path to building and maintaining courage.

   • Confidence comes from many sources, including knowing that you have a good education and training, good relationships, or even that you look good. This confidence can help bolster your courage and make you feel more willing to tackle your fears.

   • It's important to know that even if you are confident and courageous, that failure is an important part of overcoming fears and growing.

6. *Take risks and accept failure.* Part of building your courage is taking risks, some of which will be successful and others, which may fail. The ability to take a risk and accept the potential failure can significantly help to boost your confidence and courage in the future.

   • Simply stepping out of your comfort zone will help to build confidence.

   • Take calculated risks and move slowly. For example, if you are afraid of heights, start to build your courage in high places slowly. You can climb to a three-meter diving board and look into a pool or take the stairs to the top of a small building. You don't have to skydive from a plane to tackle your fear of heights and build courage.

   • Accept that there is going to be failure in any endeavor. Learning to embrace the failure and then move on can help to not undermine your courage and allow you to continue taking calculated risks.

7. *Use obstacles to your benefit.* Take obstacles that present themselves in your life and turn them into assets. This is another form of taking risks and can help to boost your courage and confidence.

- There is a famous story about Nelson Mandela who decided to change South Africa after being told by a tribal elder that his status as a second-class citizen would effectively mean he wasn't a man. Using Mandela's model of taking an obstacle and turning it into an asset can help you gain the courage to overcome your hindrances.
- For example, perhaps you have an injury that makes it difficult to take part in certain sports. Finding certain ways to modify playing a sport you want can significantly build your courage.

8. *Take the road less traveled.* Taking the road less traveled not only requires taking risks, but also having the courage to act differently than others. Standing by your convictions, even if they're unpopular, and taking unconventional paths can help increase your courage.

- For example, if you want to set up a school for children in a remote valley of Nepal instead of going to law school like your friends after college graduation, take the steps to follow your dream. It takes significantly more courage to travel your path than to do what society and friends may expect of you.

9. *Relax and have fun as much as possible.* Being able to relax and have fun in any situation can help you to build courage. Not focusing on the potential for failure and staying positive can help you be successful in any situation, which may lead to greater confidence and courage.

- One study showed that positivity, including in the form of relaxation and having fun, contributes significantly to successfully overcoming situations.

10. *Keep moving forward.* You will occasionally have negative thoughts, which is normal and acceptable, but learn not to dwell on them. By always moving toward the positive, you will be able to change your negative attitude. Remember that you need to remind you every day that you are excellent in front of your mirror.

Courage Assessment Tool

This assessment is one of possible assessments in courage and is not meant to label you as either a hero or a coward. It is merely intended to get a broad measure of how susceptible you are to fear (Part I) and how susceptible you are to bravery (Part II). Answer the following questions as honestly as possible. You will need a pen and paper for this quiz. Please respond to each statement by choosing the number from 1 to 7 that indicates how much you agree or disagree. Note down the number for each answer, and then calculate your score by following the instructions at the end of each part. At the final section I suggest how to interpret the scores.

Part 1: Your Fear Score

1. I worry about how others will view me.
   - (Strongly Disagree)
   - (Disagree)
   - (Slightly Disagree)
   - (Neutral)
   - (Slightly Agree)
   - (Agree)
   - (Strongly Agree)
2. I frequently focus on possible failure.
   - (Strongly Disagree)
   - (Disagree)
   - (Slightly Disagree)
   - (Neutral)
   - (Slightly Agree)
   - (Agree)
   - (Strongly Agree)
3. My fear of making mistakes sometimes holds me back from trying.
   - (Strongly Disagree)
   - (Disagree)
   - (Slightly Disagree)
   - (Neutral)
   - (Slightly Agree)
   - (Agree)
   - (Strongly Agree)
4. I find physical adventure intimidating.
   - (Strongly Disagree)
   - (Disagree)

- (Slightly Disagree)
- (Neutral)
- (Slightly Agree)
- (Agree)
- (Strongly Agree)

5. My worry holds me back from doing what I'd like to do.
   - (Strongly Disagree)
   - (Disagree)
   - (Slightly Disagree)
   - (Neutral)
   - (Slightly Agree)
   - (Agree)
   - (Strongly Agree)

6. The world is full of people who will take advantage of you given a chance.
   - (Strongly Disagree)
   - (Disagree)
   - (Slightly Disagree)
   - (Neutral)
   - (Slightly Agree)
   - (Agree)
   - (Strongly Agree)

7. I experience fear or worry every day.
   - (Strongly Disagree)
   - (Disagree)
   - (Slightly Disagree)
   - (Neutral)
   - (Slightly Agree)
   - (Agree)
   - (Strongly Agree)

8. I feel that if I let go of the control of projects bad things will happen.
   - (Strongly Disagree)
   - (Disagree)
   - (Slightly Disagree)
   - (Neutral)
   - (Slightly Agree)

- (Agree)
- (Strongly Agree)

9. It is usually better to play it safe.
   - (Strongly Disagree)
   - (Disagree)
   - (Slightly Disagree)
   - (Neutral)
   - (Slightly Agree)
   - (Agree)
   - (Strongly Agree)

10. I like to stick to the familiar.
    - (Strongly Disagree)
    - (Disagree)
    - (Slightly Disagree)
    - (Neutral)
    - (Slightly Agree)
    - (Agree)
    - (Strongly Agree)

For Part 1 add up your total score and write it down. *Scores below 40* suggest that you experience passing fears and that you likely do not hold yourself back in life. *Scores of 40 to 50* suggest that you experience fears that you might in some cases keep you from engaging in life in the way you would otherwise hope to. *Scores above 50* suggest that you experience a fair amount of worry, anxiety, and fear. It may or may not be severe, but it suggests there is room for growth in getting control of your own fear as you learn to be more courageous.

Part 2: Your Propensity toward Bravery

1. I take risks because they usually pay off.
   - (Strongly Disagree)
   - (Disagree)
   - (Slightly Disagree)
   - (Neutral)
   - (Slightly Agree)

- (Agree)
- (Strongly Agree)

2. I know I will be able to handle problems if they arise.
   - (Strongly Disagree)
   - (Disagree)
   - (Slightly Disagree)
   - (Neutral)
   - (Slightly Agree)
   - (Agree)
   - (Strongly Agree)

3. I don't mind a little conflict if it means doing something important to me.
   - (Strongly Disagree)
   - (Disagree)
   - (Slightly Disagree)
   - (Neutral)
   - (Slightly Agree)
   - (Agree)
   - (Strongly Agree)

4. I usually expect the best.
   - (Strongly Disagree)
   - (Disagree)
   - (Slightly Disagree)
   - (Neutral)
   - (Slightly Agree)
   - (Agree)
   - (Strongly Agree)

5. I would be willing to go skydiving or engage in another challenging behavior just to prove to myself that I could.
   - (Strongly Disagree)
   - (Disagree)
   - (Slightly Disagree)
   - (Neutral)
   - (Slightly Agree)
   - (Agree)
   - (Strongly Agree)

6. I have a history of taking on challenging projects.
   - (Strongly Disagree)
   - (Disagree)
   - (Slightly Disagree)
   - (Neutral)
   - (Slightly Agree)
   - (Agree)
   - (Strongly Agree)

7. Intense social pressure would not make me hesitant to do the right thing.
   - (Strongly Disagree)
   - (Disagree)
   - (Slightly Disagree)
   - (Neutral)
   - (Slightly Agree)
   - (Agree)
   - (Strongly Agree)

8. I would express an opinion if I thought it were correct, even if I knew it would be unpopular.
   - (Strongly Disagree)
   - (Disagree)
   - (Slightly Disagree)
   - (Neutral)
   - (Slightly Agree)
   - (Agree)
   - (Strongly Agree)

9. I would be likely to confront a parent who was yelling in a mean way at a children's sporting event.
   - (Strongly Disagree)
   - (Disagree)
   - (Slightly Disagree)
   - (Neutral)
   - (Slightly Agree)
   - (Agree)
   - (Strongly Agree)

10. If there were a medical emergency, I could be counted on to remain calm and do my part.
    - (Strongly Disagree)
    - (Disagree)
    - (Slightly Disagree)
    - (Neutral)
    - (Slightly Agree)
    - (Agree)
    - (Strongly Agree)

For Part 2 add up your total score and write it down. *Scores of 40 to 50* suggest that you tend to take appropriate risks and face challenging circumstances. *Very low scores, such as 20 to 30* suggest that you have room to grow in the courage department. Extraordinarily high scores, such as 60 to 70, should also be examined closely. Such scores might indicate that you are naturally courageous but might also indicate a tendency not to look before you leap. The bravest individuals often have to temper their courage to make sure they are using their talents wisely and not taking risks that could bring avoidable negative consequences or failure.

Computing Your Courage Quotient

When you look at your fear score and at your propensity toward bravery score, bear in mind that these are not infallible measures. They may miss out on small but important aspects of your personality and behavior. They are not meant to be read as the final authoritative word on anyone's level of courage. They are simply a psychological "snapshot" of the relative amount of internal fear you contend with on a day-to-day basis, and how accomplished you currently are at dealing with fear. Regardless of the specifics of your scores, the real magic will be in seeing how your fear score diminishes and your propensity toward bravery score increases as you read this book and apply its various techniques.

Chapter Summary

Courage does not always roar as a lion. Sometimes courage is the little voice from a mouse at the end of the day that says I will try again tomorrow. Use your courage every day as a project manager and learn a little more each day.

These are my suggested reminders for this chapter:

1. Courage is not the lack of fear, or the absence of fear is just to move forward even when you do not feel totally ready to do something new.
2. Have good courage and prosperity will come. As a consequence, then you shall have good success.
3. Courage is linked to self-confidence and that is a consequence of hard work on preparing yourself.
4. The greatest leaders do not just move past an obstacle—they find meaning in it and use it to their advantage
5. As a professional, you have to look at your weakest moments as opportunities rather than limitations.
6. But by identifying the source of any lack of courage and actively changing your behaviors, you can build confidence in any aspect of your life.
7. Assess your courage quotient and prepare your action plan to improve.

References

Bucero, A. 2010. *Today Is a Good Day: Attitudes for Achieving Project Success.* Ontario, Canada: Multimedia Publications.

Covey, S. 2004. *The Seven Habits of High Effective People.* Rosetta-book.

CHAPTER 9

Go for It!

Go for it now. The future is promised to no one.

—Wayne Dyer

How many times have you thought, "If I had done that or this I would be in other place, job, location." Complaining is one of the practices from the 21st century, but please stop complaining and take action. If you want to achieve something, prepare a plan and just do it. Do you want to pass away without doing the things, or after achieving the goals you wanted to get done? I do not think so because if not you would be reading other type of book. Today is a good day for you and tomorrow will be better if you are able to act (Bucero 2017).

Are you dreaming? I am dreaming very frequently because I strongly believe that I would need to live two hundred years at least to be able to accomplish my dreams, to help more people, to learn more, and to love people more. It is amazing the number of pending things an individual need to do in his or her life. Because of that you need to find out what you want in your life, then prepare a plan and go for it. Easy or difficult? I believe it is up to you. The first step for me is to believe that you can do it, after that you need to prepare a plan and use your passion, persistence, and patience to achieve your goal (Figure 9.1).

Do you think is it too risky? Perhaps it is but you do not know if you are able to do it till you try it. Do not be fear, try it, test it, and you will learn something new, or at least you will know that you cannot because you tried it. Other people are shy trying something new like delivering a talk not in the mother language. You need to try it because that would force you to study more that language, to practice more, to know more, and finally perhaps to talk better and better.

everything you want is outside of your comfort zone.

Facebook.com/FullLifeRevolution

Figure 9.1　Go for it!

Where Are You Going?

After many years as a project management practitioner, I decided to start writing as a project practitioner, then I started writing articles and columns, then papers, and over the years some books. I was very lucky of meeting Randall L. Englund who introduced me some magazine editors, and who taught me how to write in English. I planned for it and I went for it, and over the years I achieved my goals using my 3 Ps. I always had passion for writing and reading so I proposed myself and got it done.

Where are you going? Think about something you want to achieve professionally, gather as much information as possible regarding that, look for a mentor, plan to do it, and finally go for it. Simple but powerful steps to follow. Somebody will ask what happens if you fail in the middle of your path. My answer is that for sure you may fail sometimes, but it will be a great opportunity for you to overcome that obstacle, learn from it, and move forward. Learning from failures has been a constant in my life. I am Spanish (nobody is perfect). So, I really think that everybody could be my teacher. The nature gave us two ears and one mouth, then stop talking too much, listen more and learn more (Figure 9.2).

Figure 9.2 Listen more and learn more

As you probably have read along this book, I am on the path of achieving my PhD but my next pending thing is to become a professional speaker. Even when I am speaking in public very frequently, I did not have the opportunity to be well known in the public speaking business. Then I already took my first steps, knowing more details about that business, obtaining a public speaker certification, and so on. In a couple of years, I want to make my life from speaking engagements so I am preparing a plan for it.

Again, where are you going? Reflect upon that and work on your goal by gathering information, reading about it, looking for contacts, prepare a plan and do it. You are not losing nothing to try it, otherwise you will lose a great opportunity.

Some Suggestions to Take Action

I am a visual person, so I need to imagine (Figure 9.3) my objectives in my mind in order to accomplish them (Bucero 2017). I usually try to visualize positive images in my career and so far, I have achieved most of my goals. There are goals that take more time than others but if you have clear goals and you believe you can achieve them the only thing you need to do is to apply your passion, persistence, and patience.

Let me give you an example. I usually organize professional events in the project management field annually. I proceed as follows:

Figure 9.3 Imagination

- Assess market needs (based on the needs of customers and market to figure out the type of event that may be more attractive).
- Identify the event topic and previous content.
- *Visualize* in my mind the event success (immediately some names of the experts on the field are coming to my mind).
- Contact the experts to check previous interest in participating and ask for their professional fee.
- Prepare a business case.
- Contact the experts again to get a previous agreement on content and fee (*visualize* the success of the speakers at the event).
- Search for potential sponsors (selling the idea to sponsors very well is a key successful factor).
- *Visualize* the success again in my mind.
- Publicize an event data sheet on social media.
- Start the sales and marketing campaign.

Obviously, I am not giving you the complete details but I was just provide you an understanding of the idea that if you believe in your goals and visualize them in your mind, it will help you to create a plan to achieve it. Are you familiar with the following sentence?

"I am too busy. I don't have the time to act on my goals. Maybe I'll do later."

As I have discussed, it is just an obstacle. Luckily for us, that means it is surmountable. The mindset of "I am too busy to focus on my goals" is easily overcome with the help of some inspiration, organization, time management, and action. Of course, positive thinking will help (I believe it always helps!) but focus on doing. That is right. Do. When the busyness of your daily life shuts down the progress you want to make toward your goals, you are stuck in inaction. You are letting your thinking stop you from making progress, taking risks, and working toward dreams-come-true greatness. Adding more action will amplify your efforts and make the most of all your positive thinking.

Let me share with you nine tips (plus some bonus expertise) to ensure that your busy is bountiful:

1. *Do some matchmaking with your actions*
   I combine exercise and a commute, podcasts and preparing meals, walking while chatting with my folks. I know I write about the importance of focus and not multitasking and being present. However, there are some combinations that will give you lots of energy. You may find that listening to a digital book inspires long, inspirational walks that leave you spiritually and physically lighter.

2. *Understand your current patterns*
   Awareness is power. Think about it. Why don't you have time? Which habits are distracting and not serving you? How are you spending time in ways that are not supporting your goals? Where are you least productive and most prone to interruptions? And why? Consider tracking your busyness for a day or two to see where you experienced black holes in your time (you know, those minutes or hours that seem to have disappeared).

   Now, how can you reframe how you are spending your time? For example, your job might keep you extremely busy, but after examination, you may find opportunities to create and reserve time so you can concentrate on your goals. One of my insights is that as busier I am much more productive I will be.

3. *Make the most of little pockets of time*

For most of us, it is difficult to find a free hour or two during the day (or night, for that matter) to dedicate to something new. Your "free time" is like an unfinished crossword puzzle. The openings are here and there, and you need to be smart to fill in the open spaces. I have to boast, and I am proactive at this. I even carry around printouts of relevant articles I want to read, so that when I have five or ten minutes to spare, I can dive in and learn. It is like research on the go.

Do not be afraid to break big actions down into small actions. You can carve some unexpected chunks of time out of your day and make the most of each minute. Instead of grumbling about someone being late, think of it as a gift; you now have time to read or learn or make phone calls or develop ideas. Small steps of progress eventually equate to giant leaps closer to your goals. Down one question at a time, which made it easier later. To help set you up for success, write a list of things you can do if you had 1 minute, 5 minutes, 10 minutes, 30 minutes, or an hour. Next time you get stuck in a waiting room, you will be ready to jump into action. Please try it! The power in small, deliberate actions is unbelievable!

4. *Do not forget to recharge, re-energize and relax*

If I have a spare minute, I spend it reenergizing with some dancing, commenting on a blog by someone I admire, connecting with someone on LinkedIn, or giving my partner a one-minute, love-filled hug. Remember, you do not want to become busy being busy. You want to be productive, and you want to take action toward your goals. But you don't want to overdo it. I would recommend alternating your productive spare moments with breathing and recharging.

5. *Find your focus*

My business, Bucero PM Consulting, is a perfect example of a side project that has built up momentum with small deliberate steps. A few years ago, I was stuck in inaction with this business. I was paralyzed by too many ideas and no focus. So, I approached a coach for help and asked to set a feeling-based goal to grow Bucero PM

Consulting business enjoyably and passionately. My coach, Randy, asked me to "brain dump" all of the options and ideas I had for growing the movement. This really let me capture all my ideas—nearly 50 of them—and get them out of my head and onto paper. Then Randy had me identify which five I would focus on. Just five! I then listed the steps I needed to take for each focus. And when I didn't know what to do, the action I set was to learn what to do.

Focus was just what I needed. By setting my goal as "passionate and enjoyable," I took away the urgency or pressure I was feeling about growing the business. Since then, I have launched two sites, multiple products, and spoken at universities and businesses. All thanks to focus.

6. *Take 25*

One of my favorite tools for maximizing time is the "Pomodoro technique."[1] It's spending 25 minutes solely focused on a single task. I know what you are thinking: How much can you actually accomplish in 25 minutes? So, I challenge you: Try it. Remember, it's 25 minutes of uninterrupted productivity focused on one task. It's not 25 minutes of distracted, disrupted effortless whimsy. Concentrate!

A couple of things happen when you do. You might love it. You might love it so much that you look for more 25-minute opportunities. You may begin to shift your priorities, smash distractions, lose un-serving habits with ease—all because you saw the power of 25 minutes. I look at my own Top Five habit here: Taking a few minutes each day to reflect on positive moments has led to a collection of more than 10,000 positive memories and a movement. Greatness is just 25 minutes away.

---

[1] There are six steps in the original technique:
1. Decide on the task to be done.
2. Set the pomodoro timer (traditionally to 25 minutes).
3. Work on the task.
4. End work when the timer rings and put a checkmark on a piece of paper.
5. If you have fewer than four checkmarks, take a short break (3–5 minutes), then go to step 2.
Pomodoro Technique: Wikipedia
https://en.wikipedia.org/wiki/Pomodoro_Technique

7. *Balance collecting wisdom with taking action*

I look at advice, pearls of wisdom, routines, and tips as being tools. You need these kinds of tools to get the result you want. But not all tools are going to work for you. You just won't like some of them, some will become uncomfortable as you learn and grow, and others will inspire you to use them again and again. Savor the ones that work, but toss the ones that don't. Recognize that you can do any-thing—but not everything. Make sure those any things are making your life better or easier or more satisfying.

8. *Reframe the reasons why you are not starting now*

It just would not be a blog post from me without a bit of positive thinking. So, here goes: Life has lots of layers and complications and potential distractions. It might be the worst time to do something, or it actually might be the very best time to do it. We often think of reasons *not* to do something, but what about focusing on all the reasons why you should take action. Sometimes the toughest work is in the thinking—not the actual acting.

9. *Set boundaries*

When you say yes to yourself and your goals, it means making a commitment to setting some supportive, smart, and exciting bound-aries to create space for action. Know what you want, know how far you want to go, how much time you are willing to put in, and know what you are willing to sacrifice (and not sacrifice). When it comes to prioritizing your goals, you are in charge. Make sure you know your limits.

10. *Some more tips or suggestions*

There is so much enlightening information and expertise about this topic. I wanted to share some of my findings:

- A business coach who was working with one of my teams suggests replacing the word "busy" with "productive." His change in language is also a good reminder to check in with yourself if you are being busy or productive. It is a subtle shift in language that is both helpful and insightful.
- Check out international business philosopher Jim Rohn's speech that has been made into a video. It is called "Why Not You," and it challenges your perceptions of why you are not seizing the day.

People often say that it is not about having time, but about making time. So, let's make some time. Which of these tips/tools can you take and put into action right now? Come on, go for it!

Develop Your Willingness

According to new research, being motivated to learn new skills is the attribute, executives say, is most critical for employees looking to get ahead (Figure 9.4). Specifically, 30 percent of executives said having a willingness to keep learning is the characteristic they consider most necessary for an employee to succeed, according to the study from the staffing firm Accountemps.

I believe that successful people never stop learning. The world is changing quickly and constantly, and it is vital to stay informed of the latest trends and sought-after skills in your industry. Executives are also placing greater importance on the ability to communicate and get along with others in the workplace. I believe having strong interpersonal skills is critical to an employees' success.

Being able to adapt easily to change and welcoming increased responsibility were the other top traits the surveyed executives said are necessary for professional advancement. Least important to executives was a willingness to burn the midnight oil. Just 7 percent of those surveyed said working long hours is a necessary success strategy.

Figure 9.4 Develop your willingness

To help project professionals looking to get ahead, I would like to share the following steps:

1. *Get involved*: Joining industry associations is a good way to learn new skills and keep up-to-date on the trends affecting your profession.
2. *Volunteer*: Volunteering for a nonprofit organization can help you hone your skills. In addition, these types of experiences provide opportunities for you to grow and learn.
3. *Keep learning*: Earning an advanced degree or certification is a good way to demonstrate to employers your willingness to continue learning new skills. It also helps cement your expertise within your field.
4. *Hone your communication skills*: When communicating in the workplace, it is important to observe body language, make eye contact, and listen fully to what the other person is saying. When speaking to important audiences, it can also be helpful to rehearse what you're going to say. Those who need work on their public speaking should consider joining a professional organization like Toastmasters.
5. *Think long term*: You always want to be thinking about the big picture. This type of mindset can help you make more strategic decisions and put you in a better position to get ahead.

The study was based on surveys of more than 2,200 chief financial officers from companies in more than twenty of the largest U.S. metropolitan areas.

Willingness Assessment Tool

This is a quick test for you to self-assess your willingness to be an empowering leader, along with a key to interpret your score and decide how to follow up.

Rate yourself on each question on a 1 to 10 scale, with 1 being "Never" and 10 being "Always." Add the ratings for all questions to get your total empowering leadership score. A perfect score would be 100.

1. Do I believe in people and feel they are an organization's most appreciable asset? _____

2. Do I feel that team leadership can accomplish more than individual leadership? _____

3. Do I look for potential leaders and quickly assimilate them into the organization? _____

4. Do I desire to raise others above my own level of leadership? _____

5. Do I invest time developing people who have leadership potential? _____

6. Do I enjoy watching others get credit for what I taught them? _____

7. Do I allow others the freedom of personality and process, or do I have to be in control? _____

8. Do I give my influence publicly to potential leaders as much as possible? _____

9. Do I plan to have others take my present position? _____

10. Do I hand the leadership baton off to a teammate and truly root for him or her? _____

- *If you scored 100*, congratulations! You are an empowering leader. Commit yourself to developing leaders who empower others, as opposed to only developing followers:
  - Identify potential leaders
  - Assess their leadership talents and learning style preferences
  - Develop a plan for their growth
- *If you scored 90 to 99*, give yourself a pat on the back. You are well on your way to becoming an empowering leader. Focus on your weakest area of development. Develop a plan addressing only that skill set. Include:
  - Reading leadership articles/books specific to your area of development
  - Keep a journal of weekly activity toward improvement
  - Work with a mentor
- Reassess your rating in six months
- *If you scored 75 to 90*, you have built the foundation of effective leadership. Examine areas where you need to strengthen. Focus on your two weakest areas of development plus one area of strength. Develop a growth plan for each of the three areas, with specific milestones, to include:

- o Selected readings focused on leadership and growth
- o Three activities per week in which you specifically address each of the three areas
- o Meeting with a mentor monthly, to keep you accountable to your growth plan
- Reassess your rating in three months.
- *If you scored 50 to 74,* you are doing okay as a leader, but you have the potential to do much better. Focus on two strength areas plus one of your areas of development. Develop a growth plan, with the help of your supervisor, for each of the three areas that includes:
- o Selected readings on leadership and growth
- o Three activities per week in which you specifically address each of the three areas
- o Meeting with your supervisor weekly to assess your progress and keep you accountable to your growth plan
- Reassess your rating in three months
- *If you scored below 50,* you have a lot of work to do as a leader. The good news is you can practice these skills at work, at home and in the community. Identify your career aspirations and determine where you want to be in the next 12 to 36 months. Do your aspirations include a role as a single contributor or a leadership position?
- o Develop a career development plan with your supervisor that is focused on your career aspirations.
- Reassess your rating in 12 months

Chapter Summary

From the ideas, best practices and concepts covered in this chapter, please select the ones who may help you to move forward:

- The first step for me is to believe that you can do it; after that you need to prepare a plan and use your passion, persistence, and patience to achieve your goal.

- Reflect upon that and work on your goal by gathering information, reading about it, looking for contacts, prepare a plan, and do it. You are not losing nothing to try it; otherwise you will lose a great opportunity.
- The mindset of "I am too busy to focus on my goals" is easily overcome with the help of some inspiration, organization, time management, and action. Of course, positive thinking will help.
- Do some matchmaking with your actions, understand your current patterns, make the most of little pockets of time, do not forget to recharge, re-energize and relax, find your focus.
- Balance wisdom with taking actions.
- People often say that it is not about having time, but about making time. So, let's make some time.
- Get involved, be a volunteer, keep learning, improve your communication skills, and think a long term.
- Assess your willingness and take an action plan to improve.

Dream more and go for it! You can do it because you are excellent, you can do it only if you believe you can.

Reference

Bucero, A. 2017. *Tomorrow Will Be Better: Maintaining a Positive Attitude for Project*. Motivational Press.

CHAPTER 10

Conclusions

Go for it now. The future is promised to no one.

—Wayne Dyer

Now I hope that most the material you have read was served you at least to reflect upon and understand better who you are, and understand that if you believe in your dreams you will be unstoppable. And definitely you are. The most powerful word in my life has been and still is "thank you." I am so thankful you have read this book or part of it, because it means that you are a dreamer project practitioner like me. It has a lot of value for me because our world needs a lot of project managers who believe in the projects they manage, professionals who are passionate, persistent, and patient and are able to manage successful projects in organizations.

This book is not only about who you are today and what is the level of your passion, persistence, and patience, it is about what you can be in the near future as a project manager. The energy in our veins helps us to move forward all the time, gives us the strength to continue on any initiative we start, and in any project we manage. Welcome to my 3Ps club. You are a great professional and every day you can say "today is a good day" and you need to be convinced that "tomorrow will be better."

I told you many stories along this book, real stories that happened to me or to other project management professional colleagues. All of them are interesting stories for me because they are part of my life as a project management professional but also taught me many life lessons. Sometimes we want to know much too quickly and finally I understood that everything in life takes time, effort, and dedication. Then, be enthusiastic with your ideas and new projects, believe in them and use your passion, persistence, and patience to obtain great results.

On some occasions, you will feel like too weak to continue due to the number of obstacles to overcome. Do not allow your mind to do so; remember that you are a believer who can achieve your dreams only if you believe you can, and apply my 3Ps. From now you belong to my 3Ps club, and so never give up. We have many projects to manage worldwide and our society needs us; do not forget that. I am now in the sixth decade of my life but I still have a young heart that tells me every day "I need you. I want you and I love you." Please move forward and take action. And believe me I am committed to do it. If you need any help on that, please let me know.

Some actions that project managers need to take when managing a project

Depending on the type of organization the project manager is working for, he or she may have more responsibility than authority. Then, in order to be successful at motivating project team members and other project stakeholders in an environment where the followers do not have to do what they are told, the project manager needs to find some other method to motivate them. Applying passion, persistence and patience will be great mechanisms to get all stakeholders engaged, and participating on achieving project results from the very beginning of the project and during the whole project life cycle.

In my experience, as a project manager, I learned how to apply passion, persistence and patience along the project life cycle. Some of the issues I found happened when:

- Gaining upper management support
- Overcoming some resistance from executives, customers and other stakeholders
- Creating and maintaining a positive attitude atmosphere in every project
- Getting stakeholders engaged
- Supporting team members and other stakeholders during the whole project life cycle
- Encouraging team members commitment and participation

- Supporting people to achieve results
- Creating the teamwork spirit
- Transmitting enthusiasm to customers and other stakeholders

I am blessed because I had the opportunity to work for functional, matrix and projectized organizations as a project manager. I lived the differences among them regarding project management.

First of all, when I worked for a functional organization the main problems, I found, were based on the inexistence of the project manager role. In that organization I had no authority at all and I needed to influence without authority obtaining smaller and smaller tangible results as earliest as possible. I believe in the profession since I started as a project manager, so my first practice was showing my passion to my manager in order to demonstrate him that I would be successful managing my team and the project would be successful. Passion and persistence were used by myself when working for that functional organization. I needed to overcome executive lack of project knowledge and lack of interest.

Secondly, when working for matrix organization I had a little bit more support, my project manager role existed formally in the organization but I needed to deal with functional managers that did not believe in project management. In those organizations what I did was spending a lot of time talking to functional and upper managers and trying to get educated into the strategic part of project management. Many meetings and presentations were organized till I gained little by little some management support. I continued using passion and persistence during years although the most difficult part was using my patience. I was really impatient over several years till I learned that not all professionals work and understand project management at the same pace. I was extremely persistent on teaching and explaining them what is in it for them.

Last but not least I had the opportunity to work for a strong matrix organization that more and more was converted into a projectized organization but even in that one I needed and I need to use my passion, persistence and patience for every project I managed. Executives are more aware of the project manager role, more conscious about the need of planning but as organization I need to obtain results in the most effective way.

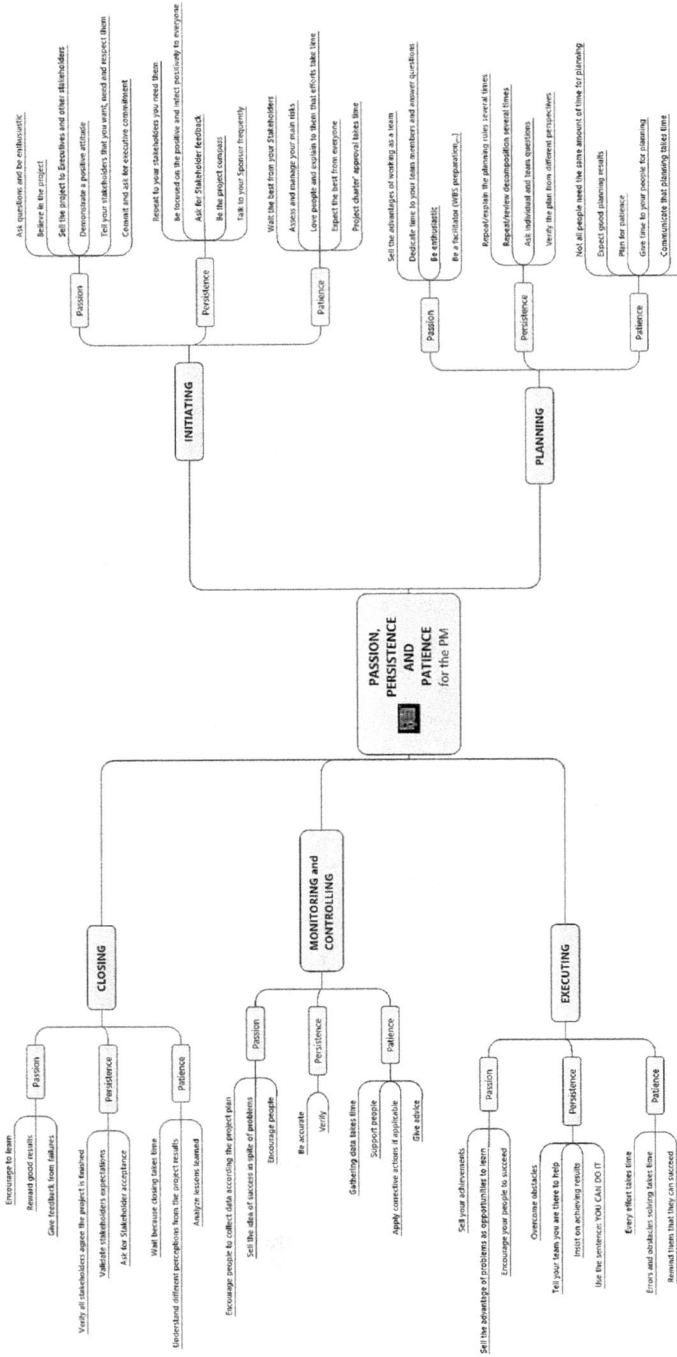

PASSION, PERSISTENCE AND PATIENCE for the PM

INITIATING

Passion
- Ask questions and be enthusiastic
- Believe in the project
- Sell the project to Executives and other stakeholders
- Demonstrate a positive attitude
- Tell your stakeholders that you want, need and respect them
- Commit and ask for executive commitment

Persistence
- Repeat to your stakeholders you need them
- Be focused on the positive and reflect positively to everyone
- Ask for Stakeholder feedback
- Be the project canvass
- Talk to your Sponsor frequently

Patience
- Wait the best from your Stakeholders
- Assess and manage your main risks
- Love people and explain to them that efforts take time
- Expect the best from everyone
- Project charter approval takes time

PLANNING

Passion
- Sell the advantages of working as a team
- Dedicate time to your team members and answer questions
- Be enthusiastic
- Be a facilitator (WBS preparation...)

Persistence
- Repeat/explain the planning rules several times
- Repeat/review decomposition several times
- Ask individual and team questions
- Verify the plan from different perspectives

Patience
- Not all people need the same amount of time for planning
- Expect good planning results
- Plan for patience
- Give time to your people for planning
- Communicate that planning takes time

CLOSING

Passion
- Encourage to learn
- Reward good results
- Give feedback from failures

Persistence
- Verify all stakeholders agree the project is finished
- Validate stakeholders expectations
- Ask for Stakeholder acceptance
- Wait because closing takes time

Patience
- Understand different perceptions from the project results
- Analyze lessons learned

MONITORING and CONTROLLING

Passion
- Encourage people to collect data according the project plan
- Sell the idea of success in spite of problems
- Encourage people

Persistence
- Be accurate
- Verify
- Support people

Patience
- Gathering data takes time
- Apply corrective actions if applicable
- Give advice

EXECUTING

Passion
- Sell the advantage of problems as opportunities to learn
- Sell your achievements
- Encourage your people to succeed
- Overcome obstacles

Persistence
- Tell your team you are there to help
- Insist on achieving results
- Use the sentence: YOU CAN DO IT

Patience
- Every effort takes time
- Errors and obstacles solving takes time
- Remind them that they can succeed

I want to say that I strongly believe that every project manager needs to discover, develop and apply his/her passion, persistence and patience for managing projects. Based on that, I elaborated the previous mind map that is showing some of my 3Ps actions to be taken at every project you managed. Please review it. I expect you will be able to reflect upon them and customize it to be used by you at every project.

Summary and Conclusions

Passion is part of my life because I am blessed with working on the field that I love, project management, on a world where project management is the need of our society, on an environment with great colleagues to learn from. I strongly believe passion makes the difference between success and failure in our lives. Passion is very important. Following your passion is the secret to overcoming the setbacks all entrepreneurs face and it builds resistance against the inevitable naysayers who will question your vision. Passion is about believing in what you do, inspiring others to believe in it, and loving why you do what you do.

Passion requires courage, even young-like energy, to keep your eyes on your goal and do all you can to achieve it. If you want to see enthusiasm as one of your goals, you also need to decide how you will measure it. When you have the facts on which factors increase passion, and why, it is time to consider the obstacles standing in the way of inspiration.

Persistence is one of my principles. It is really difficult to achieve your goals in your first try, at least for me it usually was. Being persistent is a skill that can help you to achieve a goal, get what you wish, and can even be a means by which you assert yourself in the face of stubborn or difficult people. The greater the achievement you seek, the more likely you will persist to achieve it. Persistence is important in your life. It will mark how well you accomplish tasks that you set for yourself. Those who persist end up with the health, fitness, and vitality that we were striving for in the beginning when the motivation was high and the weather warm.

Patience is sometimes the most difficult skill to develop for dreamers. Having patience means being able to wait mainly in the face of frustration or adversity. So anywhere there is frustration or adversity we have the opportunity to practice it. Patience helps us achieve our goals, and it is linked with good health. Patient people are better team members and colleagues. Patience is connected to trust, hope, faith, love, and good character.

I never forgot my father's comments and advice about life. He said life is a "quest with plenty of obstacles and tests." Then you always need to be prepared to deal with them. So far, I found my father a very wise man who always encouraged me to study, to be prepared, and to exit from time to time out of my comfort zone. And I followed his advice, they have worked for me, and that philosophy of life can be found too hard for some people or just funny for some of them. The truth is that if I had not been enthusiastic in all that I did I could not survive in our challenging world. I started to work as a little negative person till I found a manager who opened my eyes and from then on, I started to be positive most of the time. My passion, persistence, and patience are more and more needed than never. I need full energy to achieve my goals. Some people admires how I show up a lot of energy every day and it is easy to explain, it happens because my mind believes I need it. That energy maintains me alive.

Final Thoughts

From time to time, people who attend my seminars or people who I am helping to manage a project or program tell me that I have been working for almost 40 years now. They say, "Alfonso, you are closer and closer to retirement. What will you do when you are retired?"

My answer is very direct. I do not see myself retired because project management is not my profession, but it is my hobby. I enjoy practicing, coaching, teaching, mentoring, or speaking on the project management field. Then I will stop when God retires me. It is obvious that with every passing year, your physical body deteriorates, but you need to take care of yourself physically by doing some frequent exercise accommodated to your age and also do some exercises for your mind every day. I strongly believe that professionals like me with almost 40 years of experience have a lot to offer to other professionals and organizations and also have a lot to learn till the day they pass away.

I am very happy because God allowed me to give testimonial that I have gone around this earth by writing books like this. Some people ask me why am I writing books so frequently, and I answer them that it is not a merit because I love writing. It is amazing the amount of learning that I get in every book I write. Then, why stop writing? It makes no sense for me.

Please ask yourself the following question: Is every day a good day for you? I hope this book to help you to find your real happiness in project management. I wish you happy projects.

Today is a good day and tomorrow will be better!

About the Author

Alfonso Bucero, MSc, CPS, PMP, PMI-RMP, PfMP, PMI Fellow, is the founder and managing partner of Bucero PM Consulting (www.abucero. com). He managed IIL Spain for almost two years, and he was a senior project manager at Hewlett-Packard Spain (Madrid Office) for more than 13 years. Previously he worked as a project team member, team leader, and project manager for Secoinsa, Digital Equipment Corporation, and ICL.

Alfonso is a member of PMI and ALI (Professional engineering Asociation). Alfonso was the founder, sponsor, and president of PMI Barcelona, Spain Chapter, and he was an IPMA Assessor. He was a member of the Congress Project Action Team of PMI EMEA's Congresses in Edinburgh (2005), Madrid (2006), and Budapest (2007). He graduated from PMI's Leadership Institute Master Class 2007 in Atlanta at the PMI NA Global Congress. He was president of the PMI Madrid Spain Chapter for two years, served as component mentor for Region 8 South-West from 2011 to 2013 and served the PMIEF (PMI Educational Foundation) as a volunteer for two years. He received the PMI Distinguished Contribution Award in 2010 for his long and varied body of work, the PMI Fellow Award in 2011 from the Project Management Institute for his sustained contribution to the development of the profession internationally, and the PMI Eric Jenett Project Management Excellence Award on October 2017.

Alfonso has a computer science engineering degree from Universidad Politecnica (Madrid), got his MSc in project management at Zaragoza University and, is still working on his PhD at the ISM University in Lithuania. He has 36 years of practical experience and thirty of them in project management worldwide. He has managed and consulted on projects in various countries across Europe, United States, and the Middle East.

Since 1992, Alfonso is a frequent speaker at international PMI Congresses, IPMA Congresses, and PMI Seminars World. He has been a keynote speaker in several congresses worldwide. He delivers PM training and consulting services in several countries worldwide. As a "project management believer," he defends *passion, persistence, and patience* as vital keys for project success. Alfonso has been a professor for MEDIP (Master in Construction and Project Management) at the UPM in Madrid (Spain) since 2004, and for two years ago in Panama City (Panama), and was a professor and executive consultant for the Marketing and Finance Business School in Bilbao (Spain) for two years.

He authored the book *Dirección de Proyectos, Una Nueva Vision* published by LITO GRAPO Editors (2003). He contributed Chapter 7 of *Creating the Project Office* published by Jossey-Bass (2004), authored by Randall L. Englund, Robert J. Graham, and Paul Dinsmore. Alfonso coauthored with Randall L. Englund the book *Project Sponsorship* published by Jossey-Bass (2006). He authored the book *Today is a Good Day: Attitudes for Achieving Project Success*, published by Multimedia Publishing in Canada (2010). Alfonso contributed to the chapter "From Commander to Sponsor: Building Executive Support for Project Success" in the book *Advising Upwards* (2011) authored by Lynda Bourne in Australia. He also contributed Chapter 15 of the book *CIRCA 2025* written by Dr. David I. Cleland and Dr. Bopaya in 2010.

Alfonso coauthored with Randall L. Englund the books *The Complete Project Manager* and *The Complete Project Manager Toolkit* published by Management Concepts in March 2012 and got published a new version from his book *Dirección de Proyectos, Una Nueva Vision,* and the book *Hoy es un buen día* (Spanish translation from *Today Is a Good Day*).

Alfonso wrote and got published his book *The Influential Project Manager* by CRC Editors in the United States in 2015, coauthored a new version of the book *Project Sponsorship* with Randall L. Englund published by PMI on October 2015, and then wrote and got published his latest book *Tomorrow Will Be Better* by Motivational Press in 2017.

He has also contributed to professional magazines in the United States, Russia (SOVNET), India (ICFAI), Argentina, and Spain. Alfonso was a contributing editor for six years for the "Crossing Borders" column of *PM Network* magazine, published by the Project Management Institute. He was a monthly contributor for Project Connections blog and get published several project management articles in other professional magazines.

You can reach Alfonso Bucero at: alfonso.bucero@abucero.com

Index

www.ingramcontent.com/pod-product-compliance
Lightning Source LLC
Chambersburg PA
CBHW060529210326
41519CB00014B/3181